Secondary Environmental Science Methods

Musa Y. Qutub
Northeastern Illinois University

CHARLES E. MERRILL PUBLISHING COMPANY
A Bell & Howell Company
Columbus, Ohio

To my mother . . . who dedicated her life to my education.

The paper stock in this text is composed of 100% reclaimed wastepaper and is being used on an experimental basis. From an environmental standpoint, the advantages of using such paper are twofold: not only is no new wood pulp needed, but also a minimum of solid waste is left as a by-product of the milling process.

ISBN: 0-675-09068-7

Library of Congress Catalog Card Number: 72-83472

1 2 3 4 5 6 7 8 9—81 80 79 78 77 76 75 74 73

Printed in the United States of America

Preface

Teachers can make their classes interesting only if they arouse their students' interest and involve them in designing their curriculum. As a prospective teacher, you can play a part in improving the American educational system, and this book is designed to develop a creative approach.

The first chapter considers the case for environmental science. The second chapter tells you how to develop pilot units. In the third chapter, techniques of learning, especially an open-end approach, are considered. Chapter four outlines twenty suggested investigations focusing on your students' immediate environments, with the use of the self-directed approach strongly recommended.

The last chapter suggests ways of involving students in evaluating their learning, instead of leaving the evaluation largely to the teacher, on the theory that more learning would take place if students were allowed a more active part.

The appendixes will help you obtain the necessary resource materials for initiating or conducting an environmental science class or unit.

Contents

1

Have
the
Schools
Failed?

The call for environmental programs is not a result of the schools' failure as some educators are advocating. Educational reforms have been continuous since the birth of this nation. Environmental programs have always been difficult to define and to implement. Some high schools and colleges have been quick to institute programs in environmental science or environmental education. Other colleges have instituted programs in environmental studies, thus separating sciences from social studies.

Local environmental programs are being added to secondary school curriculums at a rapid pace, with a wide range of classroom materials being developed. This direction is practical because school environment varies from town to town. State and federal governments are encouraging such direction by providing funds for programs with an environmental science accent.

What is environmental science? Does it mean ecology, as some people define it, or does it mean biology or earth science? Make a list of the subjects you have studied that deal with environmental science.

Environmental science is the study of the total environment, including the surface and near-surface processes (physical, chemical, and biological) and their impact on life. The call for learning in environmental science or environmental education (at times referred to as nature study) dates back to the beginning of the century. In 1904, W. Jackman in *Nature Study* stated:

The spirit of nature study requires that the pupils be intelligently directed in the study of their immediate environment in its relation to themselves. That there shall be under the natural stimulus of the desire to know, a constant effort at the rational interpretation of the common things observed. If this plan be consistently pursued, it will naturally follow that the real knowledge acquired, the trustworthy methods developed, and the correct habits of observing and imagining formed will lay a sound foundation for the expansive scientific study which gradually creates a world picture and at the same time enables the student by means of the microscope, the dissecting knife, and the alembic to penetrate intelligently into its minute detail.[1]

Anna Comstock, writing in 1911 in her handbook of nature study, defined nature study thus: "A study of nature consists of simple, truthful observation that may like beads on a string finally be threaded upon the understanding and thus held together as a logical and harmonious whole."[2]

The method used for learning nature study was faculty psychology, or the theory of mental discipline. This theory asserts that the mind holds faculties which could be used by mental discipline to acquire knowledge. The harder the subject matter, the better the mind will be trained (examples are Latin and mathematics). Practice and continuous drill are essential and motivation is unimportant. This was at the time that John Dewey and William James were beginning to influence education. They emphasized that learning can best be done by experience. Due to the influence of these men, the mental discipline theory used in the nature study movement found greater opposition than expected and began to fade away. Then, in 1932, Gerald Craig suggested including four major areas in the curriculum: (1) kinds of living things; (2) changing earth conditions; (3) survival of plants; and (4) interdependence of living things in their environment. Some years later, in 1944, Craig pursued his thinking in his work, *Science in Childhood Education,* where he described the importance of and some of the methods for conservation of natural resources, emphasizing their impact on life.[3] Later, in the 46th yearbook of the National Society for the Scientific Study of Education, the use of natural resources in education was emphasized: "Probably no child will study science without having his ideas and attitudes on such matters as health, citizenship, or conservation modified."[4] Thus, conservation education or environmental education now took a firmer stand in the curriculum.

1. W. S. Jackman, *Nature Study,* 3rd yearbook of the National Society of the Scientific Study of Education (Chicago, 1904).

2. Anna Comstock, *Handbook of Nature Study* (Ithaca, N.Y.: Comstock Publishing Co., Inc., 1911).

3. Gerald S. Craig, *Science in Childhood Education* (New York: Bureau of Publications, Teachers College, Columbia University, 1944).

4. *Science Education in American Schools,* 46th yearbook, part I, the National Society for the Scientific Study of Education (Chicago: University of Chicago Press, 1947), pp. 35-39.

The concern for depletion of natural resources such as wildlife, water, soil, and forests was reflected in high school curriculums as far back as 1921 in Tennessee.[5] At that time the state legislature recommended that principles of conservation be taught in Tennessee schools. In 1944, eight other states passed similar recommendations.

The American Association of School Administrators expressed its deep concern about environmental survival as reflected in its 1951 yearbook, and, after discussing the problem, the Association passed a resolution which reads in part:

> Wastage of human and natural resources either by neglect or destruction robs society of its rightful potentialities for better living. In order to develop and conserve our human and natural resources, it is recommended that renewed emphasis be given in school curricula to the wise use of natural resources and development of fundamental principles of moral character and responsible citizenship and the preparation needed for everyday living as set forth in education for all American youth and life adjustment education for every youth.[6]

In 1954, the National Association of Biology Teachers, concerned about the conservation of natural resources, formed a committee that was responsible for a published handbook. In a survey of textbooks used in K-12 in conservation education, Elizabeth Hone in 1959 found that their major emphasis was renewable resources such as soil, water, plants, and animals —in other words, the emphasis was mainly on agriculture. Hone then suggested making conservation more relevant by including other problems facing society. In 1968, Mario Menesini suggested a program in environmental education which would emphasize the national parks. He outlined his plan in a program called NEED (National Environmental Education Development), which was intended to develop children's appreciation for their environment. This included interaction of the natural and social processes as illustrated in national park areas.

The movement for nature study instruction which began in the early 1900s, and the attempt to introduce conservation education courses or environmental management courses, some of which are still in existence in the schools, did not do the job. Several explanations for the failure of the movement are that courses did not take the student environment as a starting point and that the student was not involved in the courses as a learner. Also, as was indicated earlier, the courses' content was limited basically to agriculture.

5. C. E. Lively and J. J. Preiss, *Conservation Education in American Colleges* (New York: Ronald Press, 1957).

6. *Conservation Education in American Schools,* 29th yearbook, American Association of School Administrators (Washington, D.C., 1951).

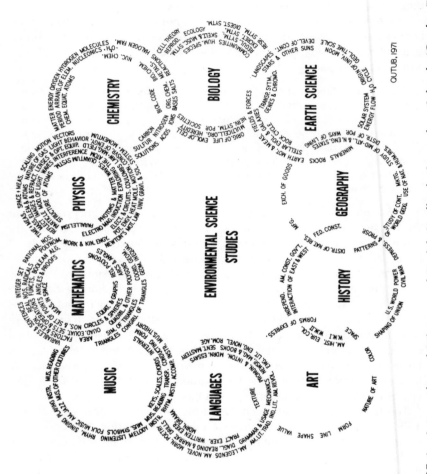

FIGURE 1.   Interaction of Science and Social Studies in Secondary Schools (Grades 7-12).

Today's environmental problems are a result of an increase in population. What is needed is not the addition of a new course to the secondary school curriculum, but a better way of humanizing the schools and restructuring the curriculums so that the student, rather than the content or the teachers, becomes the center of them. The emphasis should be on helping the student learn to solve new problems, not old ones. This can be done by starting with the student in his immediate environment. Figure 1 indicates the interaction between the sciences and the social studies in grades 7-12. What is needed is a way of showing their interrelationship. The impact of the interaction of the sciences and the social studies on man and his existence must also be shown. Whether this can be done in one course or in several courses is a question that needs to be discussed by teachers and principals. Emphasis should be on the overall structure of the curriculum.

Several questions need to be asked. Did the schools succeed in focusing the students' attention on the problems of their environment? Did the curriculum provide the student with enough experience to become aware of those problems? Did the programs developed by the science curriculum reform movement focus student attention on those problems?

Make a list of the subjects you studied in your secondary school that made you aware of the problems of your environment. Make another list of the courses you have taken so far in college that made you aware of those problems.

The American education system at the pre-college and college levels is by far one of the best in the world. The facilities available to secondary school students are conducive to learning, and the schools have been sincere about providing students with up-to-date methods and materials. However, no educational system in the world is perfect. There is always room for improvement and American schools are just now doing that. The call for environmental science is not new and should not be attributed to the failure of the schools. Even several texts currently on the market condemn the American educational system but fail to offer better solutions.

As a prospective teacher you should strive for excellence, and you can do that by understanding the operational system of the school for which you will work. If you desire to make some changes, then you must work with the system and you must work with it as a team. Science supervisors, principals, and superintendents are always receptive to new ideas, and they are making a continuous effort to improve the schools. Outline some points which should be taken into consideration when developing an environmental science program, and keep your ideas handy for your own reference when you have the opportunity to implement such a program.

City of Chicago, haze due to air pollution shown in background (Courtesy of the Department of Environmental Control, City of Chicago).

Smog over Chicago's Loop, looking southwest from the Tribune Tower (Courtesy of the Chicago *Tribune*).

Have the Schools Failed?

In developing any environmental science program and any curriculums that are K-12, several aspects of the program should be considered. First of all, the student should be the center of the curriculum. He should be encouraged to tackle real problems in his environment as much as possible through the self-directed approach.

Students, parents, and concerned members of the community and its scientists should be more involved in curriculum design. The problems of the environment should be outlined and defined. For instance, air and water pollution are only two aspects of the problems. School districts that do not have these problems should concentrate on other areas of their environment as a motive to study science concepts.

Course content development should be sequential K-12 where the school system allows it and should focus the students' attention on problems of the environment. The best place to start may be the school yard because it is a good laboratory in the natural environment.

The emphasis should not be just on ecology, soil conservation, air pollution, or water pollution. Some schools and curriculums associate ecology with environmental science, but ecology is not the only field that should be associated with it. Environmental science incorporates all of the sciences, and their impact on social studies should be made clear. Also, to come up with a truly effective program in environmental education, the curriculums should be K-12.

The school system should get its own teachers to develop a program that would fit their own needs and meet their own natural environment. The best and most immediate way is to offer environmental science as units in the sciences and the social studies in K-12, and not as a separate course.

BIBLIOGRAPHY

Hone, Elizabeth. "An Analysis of Conservation Education in Curriculums for Grades K-12." Ph.D. dissertation, University of Southern California, Los Angeles, 1959.

Landsberg, H. H. *Natural Resources for U.S. Growth.* Resources for the Future, Inc. Baltimore, Md.: Johns Hopkins Press, 1964.

Menesini, Mario M. *National Environmental Education Development.* Washington, D.C.: National Park Service, 1968.

Qutub, M. Y. "Teaching Earth Science in High School." *Science Activities* 4, no. 4 (December 1970):10-14.

———. "Environmental Programs: Status and Data." *Science Activities* 7, no. 4 (May 1972): 43-47.

2

Development
of
Pilot
Units

The reasons for stressing environmental science in secondary schools were discussed in chapter one. Secondary principals and teachers are not sure what to include in the curriculum. Some have introduced a unit, others a new course. Still others have restructured their curriculum and slanted it toward environmental science. Some have done nothing so far.

What do you think the schools should do about environmental science? Should they add a unit, a course, or a curriculum for grades 7-12? Why do you feel as you do?

As a secondary school prospective teacher, you may be called upon to participate in designing a unit, a course, or a curriculum (grades 7-12) in environmental science. This chapter will discuss ways to help you fulfill such an opportunity.

First it would be wise to review curriculum reforms that took place in the school where you are practice learning or in which you will be helping students to learn. Outline your findings. For current secondary teachers, you may review curriculum reforms in your school.

Did these curriculum reforms differ from the statewide reforms in secondary schools? Review the secondary curriculum reforms that took place in the state in which you will be helping students to learn or in your state. Make an outline of your findings.

The American Secondary Science Curriculum was influenced by national events which are summarized as follows.

1635–1751   The first American secondary school was formed, its aim being to prepare students for college. The first Academy

9

was also formed. The goal of education was to prepare students for life. Colleges influenced the secondary school curriculum during this period.

1752–1827 The first school for girls was opened, and the first public high school was organized to prepare students for life. During 1827, in Boston, Massachusetts, a law was passed requiring every community of 500 families to set up a high school. Other states followed. The curriculum included English, grammar, geometry, arithmetic, surveying, algebra, reading, writing, orthography, and history of the United States.

1828–1870 High school accreditation was granted in Michigan by a university and other states followed with similar actions.

1871–1890 The Supreme Court of the state of Michigan ruled in the *Kalamazoo* case in favor of spending funds for support of secondary education. Similar action followed in other states. The first regional accreditation association for high schools was established and enrollment began to double every decade from 1890 to 1930.

1891–1900 The Committee on Secondary Schools Studies (known as the Committee of Ten) investigated high school curriculum and grouped the subjects as follows: math, English, Greek, Latin, physics, astronomy, chemistry, natural history (botany, biology, physiology, zoology), history, civil government and political economy, geography (physical geography, geology, metrology). The main emphasis was that learning should be useful to life and the approach to learning should be through the discipline of the mind. John Dewey's philosophy began to influence the high school curriculum.

1902–1919 The first junior college was formed (Joliet, Illinois) and secondary education was extended to the 13th and 14th grades. The Smith-Hughes Act was the first federal government support for vocational education. The National Education Association urged schools to plan their programs to meet the entrance exams for college and to modify their curriculum to meet student needs. The commission on reorganization of secondary education produced the Cardinal Principles which listed seven objectives of secondary education: Health, Command of Fundamental Processes, Vocation, Worthy Home Membership, Worthy Use of Leisure, Civic Education, and Ethical Character. The Progressive Education Association was organized to unite experimental programs in secondary schools.

1920–1940	Admission of high school students to colleges on the basis of grades was weakened by the Pennsylvania study which revealed a wide range of ability groups. The Progressive Education Association began an eight-year study to determine if the subjects included in the high school curriculums were essential to college. The study revealed that certain subjects had no direct value in preparing students for college.
1960	A study conducted by the Office of Education revealed that 40 percent of high school students completed vocational programs. The remaining 60 percent did not receive adequate education. Other studies followed and the National Citizen Committee was organized which brought more support for the high schools. Audiovisual aids began to be used in the high schools. The Supreme Court decided that segregation of the races was unconstitutional. Schools began to be consolidated and the small schools began to disappear. College courses were introduced to superior high school students. Federal support for education took a firmer stand by passing the National Defense Education Act. Parents, scientists, psychologists, and others criticized the quality of education being offered to their children. Handicapped students received more attention and financial support.
1961–1970	Enrollment increased on a larger scale. A wave of science curriculum reforms began supported largely by the National Science Foundation. Several schools offered courses in world cultures, world geography, and history of nonwestern nations. The first revision of NSF curriculums took place.
1972–	The demand for environmental science programs became stronger. Curriculum revisions became imminent. Several schools introduced a unit or a course in environmental science. School busing became a major issue. Science enrollment in the secondary schools decreased rapidly. Science requirements were being minimized. Federal and state spending on secondary education was reduced. Students demanded curriculums that were relevant to their daily lives.

Did any of the national events that shaped the secondary school curriculum affect your school? Or your state? If so, how? How does the curriculum revision through the years differ in your state from the national effort to revise the curriculum? After reviewing the history of secondary science curriculum reforms in your state and at the national level, do you see any trends, patterns, or cycles?

Efforts to improve the science curriculum at the secondary level seem to occur in a cycle which began by accrediting the high schools in Michigan by the state university. Other states followed and this gave the colleges strong influence on the high school curriculum. Then in 1893, the Committee of Ten established by the National Education Association suggested that secondary education should be limited to the few that could gain by it and stressed college preparatory courses. The public became concerned about science subjects offered at the secondary level. The committee on the economy of time in education was organized in 1911 to look into the scientific value of subjects offered in the high school curriculum. This was the first scientific committee to review the high school curriculum. In 1918, the Cardinal Principles stressed that secondary education should concentrate on preparing students for a worthy life. The responsibility of the curriculum shifted from the college professors and content specialists to the schools. The superintendent appointed committees to suggest curriculum guides and laboratory investigations. Although new curriculum guides and laboratory materials were written, very few reached the teacher and the emphasis turned to improving the teacher's background. Intensive in-service programs were launched to re-train teachers. The responsibility of revising the science curriculum shifted to elected teachers who wrote new curriculum guides and laboratory investigations. Apparently, this was not enough and some criticism was directed toward science programs being offered at the secondary level. In the late 1950s, the National Science Foundation was established and the launching of Sputnik I and II in 1957 and 1958 led parents, educators, and scientists to be concerned about the nature of the science curriculum at the secondary level. As a result, the science curriculum reform movement began and the curriculums were primarily written by college faculty who dictated what was to be learned at the secondary level. The programs developed were largely funded by the National Science Foundation. They were then revised and the second generation NSF textbooks appeared but criticism still came from the schools and the teachers. Recently the emphasis seemed to shift to the schools with interest focused on local programs tailored to meet student needs and interests. The superintendents and principals appointed committees to revise existing curriculum and to produce materials that could be used at the local level with major emphasis on environmental problems.

The success of any environmental science program being planned or being conducted at the secondary level must depend on a change in the teacher's attitude. Otherwise, such programs will have little success. Curriculum changes at the secondary level are taking several forms. You may be called upon to serve on a committee formed to revise the curriculum in your school. This will entail changing certain aspects of the curriculum without changing the fundamental organization. It may require a change in the entire curriculum, its objectives, attitudes, and goals. Any curriculum change will include a change in ideas, including a change in the basic philosophy of learning and of the curriculum content as well as a change in the ideas and principles upon which this curriculum is founded. Change in attitudes is extremely vital but it has been largely ignored in previous curriculum revisions, both local and national. Regardless of whether you are changing the curriculum or improving it, one element should be emphasized: The student's interests must be assessed and considered, otherwise, the curriculum may not survive. Students who have not responded to the curriculum in the past have been considered slow-learners. This happened because others outlined the course objectives for them. Students, therefore, should be encouraged to outline their own interests and objectives and suggest ways of achieving them.

Select a secondary school science curriculum and analyze its organization and content. Make an outline of your findings.

A curriculum may be defined as a scheme to help students improve their lives and contribute to society. It should contain:

1. The course content to be studied during the academic year. It should reflect the needs of the school, the community, and the facilities available.
2. An outline of its objectives. These should be concise, clear, and reflect the interests and needs of the students.
3. Methods of learning that will be used to implement it.
4. The evaluation techniques for determining the achievements of the curriculum.

If you were asked to develop a unit in environmental science, what procedure would you follow? Outline the steps you would follow in organizing such a unit. If your school is reluctant to add a new course in environmental science, it would be advisable first to introduce and to test a unit. The success of that unit will encourage you and other teachers to participate in developing similar units. To develop a unit, you must keep in mind that environmental science includes an aggregation of scientific and social disciplines. The following suggestions will aid you in developing a unit.

1. Find out what attracts and interests your students. Keep in mind materials they come in touch with daily. For example, is the school next to a lake, a factory, or a weather station?

13

2. Make a survey of the facilities in your school. Do you need any new equipment? Can you borrow some from other departments? If you develop a unit requiring considerable expense, will your school administration approve it?

3. Outline the procedures you want to follow to implement a unit. If you are going to use the process-managerial approach for this unit, specific objectives should be outlined. But, if the students are to work on their own, ask them to outline their own objectives. One objective, for example, would be to help students recognize unsolved problems in their city and suggest solutions to them. Another would be to make students aware of population growth in their city. A third objective would be to make the students aware of water resources available in their community and how these resources are being depleted with the increase of industry and population. The unit you want to develop should be interdisciplinary and designed to be used with the current curriculum in the sciences and/or the social studies.

4. Outline the experiences to be gained from this unit. If you want students to use the process-managerial method, you will want to outline your experiences and the experiences they will gain from this unit. But, if you want them to use the self-directed method, you will want to emphasize their experiences rather than yours. In this case, the teacher will add his experiences to enrich what the students have discovered.

5. Select the content to be used in this unit. Here again, if students are investigating it on their own, they will outline the content with your help. If you are using the process-managerial method, you will want to outline the content and to guide the students to make sure they cover the materials. The emphasis should be on making the students aware of the environmental problems facing them and their city.

6. Survey the natural resources in your community, especially items that students come in contact with daily.

7. Try to survey the industries in your town and see if they are willing to conduct tours. Take students to the factories so they can become familiar with the natural resources being utilized. Try to anticipate social problems and issues which may arise in the community following student investigation.

8. Organize the content from simple to complex if you are using the process-managerial method, but if you are using the self-directed method, let students organize the content according to their interests.

9. Help students select and organize the learning experiences to be gained from this unit and ask them how they can put them to use so they can better serve their city. The learning experiences can best be outlined by the learners rather than the teacher and here a feeling of trust should develop between the teacher and the students.

10. Evaluation methods should be based on the objectives outlined for the unit and the method of learning used. Students should be asked to evaluate themselves and encouraged to demonstrate what they have gained from the unit and how they can put it to use.

This unit should be considered as a guideline possibly leading to more units to better serve the needs of the students. Every effort should be made to interest students in science.

It is imperative that teachers concerned about environmental science get together and agree on strategy for changing the curriculum. Unfortunately, teachers are slow in changing their attitudes. Will you be willing to change your attitude toward learning? Will you be willing to change a method of learning that you have used for years? Make a list showing ways you would change your attitude toward helping students learn in the classroom. Then make another list showing ways in which you would help other teachers change their attitudes.

Changing the curriculum in the secondary schools will require a designed strategy. Can you think of a procedure you would want to follow to change the curriculum in a secondary school? If you are a prospective teacher, you may want to use the school at which you have done your practice learning. If you are a teacher, you will want to change the curriculum of your own school to make it environmentally oriented. List the steps you would follow in such a curriculum change.

If a group of teachers in your school are concerned about changing the curriculum, they may want to use the following guide lines.

Developing Pilot Units

The initial step in changing a curriculum is to develop a pilot unit for use in one of your classes. The unit should be interdisciplinary in nature, environmentally oriented, and based on resources available in the community. In order to produce such a unit, classroom facilities, attitudes of teachers, school facilities, and natural resources in the community should be surveyed and objectives of the unit should be outlined. Here are some suggested objectives:

Development of Pilot Units

1. Students should recognize that our planet is dynamic and that very little has been done to explore it.
2. Students should be able to recognize the interplay of technology and society.
3. Students should recognize that change occurs constantly on our planet.
4. Students should gain an understanding of the scientific concepts and their impact on society.
5. Students should be able to recognize and suggest possible solutions to environmental problems in their community.
6. Students should be made aware of and concerned about the renewable and nonrenewable resources.
7. Students should learn to conserve the natural resources.
8. Students should be able to apply what they have studied to the community.
9. Students should be able to relate and interrelate scientific concepts that they have studied.
10. Students should be able to work, communicate, and relate to other students.

Testing the Unit

Testing will depend on the nature of the unit developed and the method of learning used (the process-managerial, self-directed, or a combination of other methods). Testing can take a year or two, or perhaps only two months. The teachers should develop a model for testing the unit based on the objectives outlined. If the self-directed method is used, students should be involved in the evaluation and should outline their own objectives. After the test is made, the weak points should be observed. Then the unit should be revised and the objectives made clear. The method of procedure and evaluation should be included in the revision. Once the unit is revised and developed and the content examined, the material should be ready for use and can be incorporated into the curriculum.

BIBLIOGRAPHY

Alberty, Harold B., and Alberty, Elsie J. *Reorganizing the High School Curriculum.* 3rd ed. New York: Macmillan, 1962. Chaps. 5-7.

Anderson, V. E. *Principles and Procedures of Curriculum Improvement.* 2d ed. New York: The Ronald Press, 1965. Chaps. 12-13.

Association for Supervision and Curriculum Development. *Role of Supervisors and Curriculum Director in a Climate of Change,* Yearbook, 1965. Washington, D.C.: The Association, 1965.

Barnes, F. P. "The Illinois Curriculum Program." In H. J. McNally and H. Passow, *Improving the Quality of Public School Programs: Approaches to Curriculum Development,* pp. 113-65. New York: Teachers College, Columbia University, 1960.

Berman, Louise M. *New Priorities in the Curriculum.* Columbus, O.: Charles E. Merrill, 1968.

Cay, D. F. *Curriculum: Design for Learning.* Indianapolis: Bobbs-Merrill, 1966. Chaps. 10-11.

Clark, L. H. et al. *The American Secondary School Curriculum.* New York: Macmillan, 1965. Chaps. 8-17.

Doll, Ronald C. *Curriculum Improvement: Decision-Making and Process.* Boston: Allyn and Bacon, 1964.

Douglass, H. R., ed. *The High School Curriculum.* 3rd ed. New York: The Ronald Press, 1964. Chaps. 9, 15-25.

Frymier, Jack R. *The Nature of Educational Method.* Columbus, O.: Charles E. Merrill, 1965.

Gilchrist, Robert S., ed. *New Curriculum Developments.* Washington, D.C.: The Association for Supervision and Curriculum Development, 1965.

Goodlad, John I. "Educational Change: A Strategy for Study and Action." *The National Elementary Principal* 48, no. 5 (1969):6-13.

Gwynn, J. Minor, and Chase, John B., Jr. *Curriculum Principles and Social Trends.* 4th ed. New York: Macmillan, 1969.

Heath, Robert W., ed. *New Curricula.* New York: Harper and Row, 1964.

Herrick, Virgil. *Strategies of Curriculum Development.* Columbus, O.: Charles E. Merrill, 1969.

Inlow, G. *The Emergent in Curriculum.* New York: John Wiley, 1966. Chaps. 7, 11, 14, 16.

King, Arthur R., Jr., and Brownell, John A. *The Curriculum and the Disciplines of Knowledge.* New York: John Wiley, 1966.

Klohr, Paul R., and Frymier, Jack R. "Curriculum Development: Dynamics of Change." *Review of Educational Research* 33, no. 3 (1963):304-21.

Krug, Edward A. *The Secondary School Curriculum.* New York: Harper and Row, 1960. Chaps. 7, 8.

Leonard, J. P. *Developing the Secondary School Curriculum.* rev. ed. New York: Holt, Rinehart & Winston, 1953. Chaps 1-9.

McKenzie, G. N., and Bebell, C. "Curriculum Development." *Review of Educational Research* 21 (June 1951).

McNally, Harold J., and Passow, A. H. *Improving the Quality of Public School Programs: Approaches to Curriculum Development.* New York: Teachers College Press, 1960.

Massialas, B. G., and Zevin, J. *Creative Encounters in the Classroom—Teaching and Learning through Discovery.* New York: John Wiley, 1967.

Miles, Matthew B., ed. *Innovations on Education.* New York: Teachers College Press, 1964.

Miller, Richard I., ed. *Perspectives on Educational Change.* New York: Appleton-Century-Crofts, 1967.

Parker, J.C. et al. *Curriculum in America.* New York: Thomas Y. Crowell, 1962. Chaps. 6-13.

Development of Pilot Units

Passow, A. Harry, ed. *Curriculum Crossroads.* New York: Teachers College Press, 1962.

Rice, J. P. "Total Talent Development." *Journal of Secondary Education* 42 (January 1967): 12-16.

Romnie, S. A. *Building the High School Curriculum.* New York: The Ronald Press, 1954. Chaps. 2-4, 7.

Rosenbloom, P. C., ed. *Modern Viewpoints in the Curriculum.* New York: McGraw-Hill, 1964. Parts III-IV, VI-VII.

Russell, James E. *Change and Challenge in American Education.* Boston: Houghton Mifflin, 1965.

Saylor, J. Galen, and Alexander, William M. *Curriculum Planning for Modern Schools.* New York: Holt, Rinehart & Winston, 1966.

Smith, B. Othanel; Stanley, William O.; and Shores, J. Harlan. *Fundamentals of Curriculum Development.* rev. ed. New York: Harcourt, Brace and World, 1957.

Taba, Hilda. *Curriculum Development Theory and Practice.* New York: Harcourt, Brace and World, 1962.

Tanner, Daniel. *Schools for Youth—Change and Challenge in Secondary Education.* New York: Macmillan, 1965. Chaps. 6, 7, 8.

Trump, J. Lloyd, and Miller, Delmas F. *Secondary School Curriculum Improvement.* Boston: Allyn and Bacon, 1968.

Tyler, Ralph E. *Basic Principles of Curriculum and Instruction.* Chicago: University of Chicago Press, 1950.

Unruh, Glenys, ed. *New Curriculum Developments.* Washington, D.C.: Association for Supervision and Curriculum Development, 1965.

Wiles, K. *The Changing Curriculum of the American High School.* Englewood Cliffs, N.J.: Prentice-Hall, 1963. Chaps. 6, 8.

3

Techniques
of
Learning

Through the ages, educators have been searching for effective methods of learning science. It is not known how the mind functions and what controls it; how students react and learn in different situations, and under what conditions they learn best. There are various schools of thought on this. Some believe students learn best by the lecture method. Others favor the inquiry or self-directed approach. Still others use a combination of various methods. And there are those who say students learn regardless of what method is used.

Students in the K-12 grades and even in college have different interests. In a class of thirty students, for example, there probably are thirty different interests, and too frequently the schools have not concerned themselves with students' interests. Thus, the didactic method is the one most commonly used. Instead, teachers should be flexible enough to use different methods in order to communicate with more students instead of a limited few, since not all students learn from the same approach. This chapter, therefore, will suggest various methods of learning environmental science, and their advantages and disadvantages.

What do you think are characteristics of good learning? What, in your opinion, are the characteristics of the successful teacher? List the characteristics of a good teacher that you had in high school. Then make a list of the characteristics of a teacher you disliked in high school and your reasons for this dislike.

The Didactic Method

In this approach the teacher identifies the concepts and the facts to be learned based on summaries and conclusions of others. He then presents them to the students. At the end of a week or a month, the teacher gives the students a test and the information is fed back to him. Construct a model for this method. Keep in mind items like content, teacher, student, evaluation, application, and others.

Why is this method of learning still so widely used all over the world, even though it is the most criticized method? Try to think of some advantages for the didactic approach to learning.

Advocates of this method argue that it is the most effective one for learning in large classes and for disseminating a large amount of information to the student. They also believe it is an easy way of transmitting an account of scientific achievements in a given discipline.

Here the teacher is the master in the class, identifying what is to be learned and how it is to be learned without regard for the needs or interests of the students. Thus, the teacher usually covers what he wishes, even disregarding some theory or information with which he may disagree although it may be relevant to the lecture.

Even though the didactic method is being used in K-12 and even in graduate schools, it is severely criticized by educators who have tried to get away from it. Can you think of reasons why this is not a good method to use in secondary schools? Try to list some disadvantages that you can think of based on courses you have taken in high school or in college which would be applicable for use with some modifications in secondary classes.

Secondary school teachers still favor the didactic or authoritarian approach probably because they have never experienced a method that does not support the idea that textbooks and teachers represent the final truth. Didacticism and science never have gone hand in hand because science questions things. Progress cannot be made in science unless we question things and seek new solutions to problems that affect our environment. The following are disadvantages of the didactic approach:

1. It leaves little room for imagination or inquiry, thus encouraging laziness and possible damage to the intellect.
2. It fails to consider the student's interests and permits the teacher to lecture on a subject that is neither timely nor within the area of the student's interest.
3. Communication is limited to the few students who may be interested in everything the teacher has to say.

4. It does not involve students in science as a method of learning. Students are not invited to make their own classifications, but are asked to memorize a ready-made chart and classifications.
5. It does not permit students to experience procedures scientists went through to discover the unknown. Instead, it tells the students how scientists made their discoveries.
6. Under this method, the course usually is structured, permitting the teacher to discuss areas of interest to himself, not to the students.
7. It encourages the student to memorize, because the material usually is presented in a way that will require a recall of terminology, drill and practice, and, therefore, the student is required to master the content being presented.
8. It leaves little room for evaluation, other than exams. The teacher decides whether the students have learned anything after covering the course material.
9. It does not offer the student the freedom to select the content of the course or to decide what he wants to learn and how he wants to learn it.
10. It does not train the mind to question things. Therefore, the mind becomes passive. When the student later is confronted with problem-solving situations, he will be uncomfortable and untrained.
11. The teacher usually asks the questions, giving very little freedom to the student to do so.

Some teachers find themselves in a situation that does not allow them to use anything but the didactic method, perhaps because of a principal's decision. In such a case, how can the lecture method be improved? How can it be used to focus the student's attention on the problems of his environment? Can you think of some ways? Write out some techniques for improving the lecture method.

If the school system in which you are helping students to learn does not allow you to use any method but the didactic, here are some suggestions for improving it:

1. Ask the students at the beginning of the year to list topics of interest to them. Use these topics as the course outline.
2. If the students cannot suggest any topics, then you make up a list of topics that deal with the environment and include concepts in science such as time, space, matter, motion, force, and energy as well as topics that will remove the barriers between the sciences and the social studies. After you have made such a list, have the students check the areas of greatest interest to them and use their recommendations in outlining the course for the year.

Make a list of topics in the field in which you will be working, such as biology, chemistry, earth science, or social studies. Outline timely topics that deal with science and social studies that you want to give your students at the beginning of the year.

3. Try as much as possible to take your students out into the field. If that isn't at all possible, give them assignments that they can do at home. For example, ask them to supply evidence of waste in their neighborhood or their environment, or examples of the effect of pollution on their environment.

4. Have one class per week during which students can ask questions pertaining to the environment. Encourage class discussion and interaction. Ask students who are passive in class for their opinions so they can interact with the rest of the class.

     After students raise questions, have them arrange themselves in small discussion groups (three to five per group). This reduces the risk for the passive student. Then a representative can report the group's ideas and decisions.

5. Invite speakers or distinguished persons from your community to discuss environmental deterioration, and what is being done to combat pollution, preserve the natural setting, and make proper use of the community's natural resources.

6. Encourage students to read newspapers and magazines and discuss what they have read in the classroom.

7. Select a popular topic such as the population explosion for the students to research and then debate in class with one group arguing for birth control, another arguing against it.

8. Select such topics as air and water pollution and suggest in lecture that air pollution is just a myth. Then allow the students to ask questions and offer opposite views.

9. Allow ten or fifteen minutes in every class to discuss what has appeared in the newspapers or on television about the environment and try to relate it to your class.

10. Approach your principal about combining the lecture method and the self-directed method for the year's program. If the principal agrees with you, you can lecture half the year and have the students work on topics that interest them the other half.

11. Select a panel consisting of a social studies teacher, a physicist, a chemist, a biologist, an earth scientist, and a geographer and have them discuss such timely topics as exploration of outer space, pollution, or waste in your community and ways of combatting them.

12. Ask your students to make a daily list of the things they did to combat pollution and preserve their environment. Read this daily list once a week or keep it on file for later comparison to see how students are progressing. Try to involve the students' parents in this matter.

13. Try whenever possible to have your lectures lab-oriented by asking students to bring things from their environment. You might assign students as a class to bring fifteen samples of plants or ten minerals or ten rocks from their community. Work with them to classify these things and determine their use.

14. Use as many visual aids as possible, including transparencies and films which relate to the environment.

15. Encourage students to bring slides they or their parents have taken on field trips. Encourage students to bring pictures they have taken that show evidence of waste or energy transfer, such as transportation of sediments, erosion, and pollution.

16. Suggest that the class form a committee that may complain to you about your presentations in class and your indifference to interests. This will establish better communications with your students and keep you aware of their interests.

   Although you will still be lecturing, you will be giving the students some voice in the content of the course.

The Process-Managerial Method

In this method of learning, the teacher identifies the concepts, skills, and objectives he wants his students to achieve. He directs them through the process of inquiry to reach these objectives. With this method, the teacher serves as both a resource person and a manager. Think of some of the advantages and disadvantages of using this method in secondary classes.

In using the process-managerial approach, several advantages can be cited.

1. The students have more freedom than in the lecture approach because they will select their own ways of solving the problems and will collect their own data and even outline the problem.

2. The student has more freedom of movement in the class where before he could only answer the teacher's questions.

3. Students will learn to support their own statements with data they have collected.

4. Students will become curious and develop an appetite for knowledge. A student attempting to solve a problem will find that there are related problems, and this discovery will lead him to new materials.

Here are some disadvantages of the process-managerial approach:

1. It is structured so that the student can follow the scope and sequence the teacher has set up for him. This has its faults because students by nature are not sequential and sequential curriculum may not be applicable to all of them.
2. The teacher has to keep asking key questions, instead of permitting the students to ask the questions.
3. In the process-managerial approach, the students usually need more time to collect and analyze their data, reach some conclusion, and relate their findings to some other areas. Slow students might not proceed as fast as the teacher would like.
4. Since the course is structured and the teacher must follow the lab investigations, the inquiry approach requires equipment that needs to be replaced from time to time.

The curriculums advocated by the science curriculum reform movement used the process-managerial approach. Some proponents claimed they were using it but that teachers, generally speaking, did not do a good job of implementing it in the schools.

Teachers need to restructure the conceptual and behavioral objectives. For example, in a biology class, one objective would be to become familiar with the types of trees, minerals, and other natural resources in the community. The content material would be found in the regular science or social studies textbooks, which the teacher would have to restructure to focus the students' attention on their own community.

Take a science or a social studies textbook in your field that uses the inquiry approach. Write the content of the conceptual and behavioral objectives, then restructure them.

After you have done this with a chapter or two, you will find it easy as you become aware of how you can implement it in your class. As much as possible, use interdisciplinary concepts and objectives to which the students can relate, and interrelate science concepts with social studies and with the community as a whole.

Open Process-Managerial

Suppose, for example, in an earth science class the students are studying the classification of soils and their mineral content. If a student becomes interested in investigating the origin of the soil, the teacher should encourage him to do so. This then becomes the open process-managerial method, with the student reporting back to the teacher, who can encourage him by asking him to report to the class about his findings. This may encourage other students to do the same thing. Thus, a teacher's objectives should be flexible enough so that he can move in the same direction as the student.

If your students seem interested in this type of approach and are doing very well on their own, this might determine how you can help your students learn for the rest of the year. This method is applicable not only to superior students, but also to slow students with reading problems.

At all times, the teacher should remember that students learn what they want to learn. If they are not interested in a given subject, they will merely go through the motions of learning and will not benefit much from it.

The Self-Directed Method

In this method of learning, the students make their own curriculum. That is, they select the content of the course to fit their interests and needs. At the beginning of the year, the teacher asks the students to indicate the area they are interested in, then he allows them to determine their own procedures and objectives. The teacher merely serves as a resource person in the class. An ideal situation would be one in which the teacher selects an area of interest to him that he can investigate in depth along with the students. This course deviates from traditional learning methods because the courses are not structured or sequential. In this method of learning, discipline problems may disappear because students are interested in what they are investigating and are, therefore, free from frustration.

Some individual teachers are experimenting with the self-directed approach, as in the North Dakota elementary schools. This method is also used extensively in England. More schools should institute experimental programs to find out what is best suited for students in a given locality. However, for the self-directed method to be effective, it should be part of the school system, not just used in one course.

To plan a lesson using the self-directed method, the teacher should ask students to indicate what topics they are interested in. If the students do not respond, the teacher should make a list of timely interdisciplinary topics that are likely to interest them as a guide. The teacher plays an important role in this self-directed method by supplementing the students' findings and encouraging them to talk about their investigations. But talking about them is not enough; he should direct and encourage them to study about other areas of interest. The personality of the teacher, therefore, is a major factor in the success of the method. If he does not have a pleasant personality and is not friendly with the students, he may have a difficult time with this method.

Using this approach to learning, the teacher should do the following:

1. Show the students how to use the equipment, which would be expensive to replace.

2. He should encourage students to collect data from their natural environment, not merely rely upon information in the library. The natural environment should be their laboratory.

3. The teacher should develop strategy that would lead students to investigate other concepts in science through key questions. For example, if in an earth science class a student is interested in investigating marijuana, the teacher should not prevent his doing this simply because it is not related to earth science per se. Marijuana is something the students come in contact with in high school, so they should be allowed to investigate it. After a few days, the teacher might ask the student about his findings. The following dialogue might occur between student and teacher:

    Teacher: Where and how do you think marijuana grows?
    Student: I don't know.
    Teacher: Do you think it will grow in soil in which it is planted?
    Student: Yes.
    Teacher: Do you think the type of soil has any impact on the type of marijuana?
    Student: Yes, I think so.
    Teacher: Do you think the type of climate has any significance on the type of marijuana produced?
    Student: I don't know. It might.
    Teacher: Well, it would be interesting to find out. Perhaps we can determine that from the references you have investigated. Or maybe you would like to do this on your own. I would be interested in your findings, and I am sure other students in this class and in the school would be too.

From types of soils and their formation, the student might go on to a study of rocks and their formation and the rock cycle. This might lead him to study about the water cycle because erosion takes place at the interface between the atmosphere, lithosphere, and hydrosphere. Eventually he might study the origin of the universe.

It is important to emphasize here that the focus does not have to be on earth science topics if it is a class in earth science or on chemistry topics if it is a chemistry class. The barriers between subjects in the sciences and the social studies should be removed. If a student in chemistry or in physics is interested in studying about population, he should be allowed to do so, and the teacher, through questioning, can lead him to study topics in physics and in chemistry.

4. The teacher should develop a model for class observation as part of his evaluation method. The student has outlined his own objectives and he should be graded on these objectives; therefore, the teacher must develop a new method of evaluation.
5. Teachers should devote more time to students on an individual basis. Every student is learning separately, although he is interacting with other students.
6. Teachers should develop a strategy for students to interact with each other. The students learn from interaction and from playing games. When a high school teacher in a suburb of Chicago was asked about the self-directed approach, he said, "I tried it and the students just played, they didn't study." He failed to see that while students are playing they are also learning, that learning can take place in many ways, not just through the structured method he was used to.
7. The teacher should create an atmosphere conducive to learning. He should help those who need help; some students who lack self-confidence because the method is new to them might be reluctant to tackle it.

List topics dealing with environmental science that you would like to present to your students for them to investigate in depth. Some teachers oppose this method of learning. Do you have any reasons that would prevent you from using it in your classes?

Traditionalists have generally opposed this method of learning and discourage its use in their schools simply because it is new. They offer the following arguments:

1. Students cannot decide for themselves and do not know what they want to study.
2. This method has yet to prove itself; there is not enough data to assure its success in the schools.
3. It requires more of the teacher's time, and sometimes, because of his heavy load, more time than he can possibly give.

4. The self-directed method is not an economical one to use in the schools, since more teachers will be needed. Using the didactic method, a teacher can handle thirty-five to forty-five students in a class.
5. Students will not cover the topics they usually cover by the lecture method. They may investigate only a single area, thus limiting their background.
6. Evaluation techniques are lacking; the students' work cannot be evaluated effectively by giving exams.
7. Parents may be passive about the method, and schools in general are not ready for the change.

On the other hand, those who have used the self-directed method successfully cite the following advantages:

1. The student will learn from his own experience, and what he learns will stay with him longer.
2. The students' interest can be used as a motivation technique to guide them to study about their natural environment, starting with their community and going on to study other concepts and their relationship to the natural setting.
3. The teacher will learn along with the students, often finding himself in a situation where he must investigate an area outside his field in order to communicate better with the students about their findings.
4. This method allows fast and slow learners to proceed according to their own speed. It also provides for those who can work with their hands and have hidden talents that are not developed by other means of learning.
5. It forces the student to think of procedures and to train his mind to solve problems with which he comes in contact.
6. It removes the barriers between the sciences and the social studies at a critical time.

The students need to report to the class periodically on their findings. They also must keep a record of what they have been doing and in a final report tell the rest of the class about their conclusions so they can move on to another problem. The teacher must try to make this a student project, serving as a resource person and guide.

Resource material that the class has—the lab, the school library, the audiovisual department—should all be made available to the students. Students should also be encouraged to go to chemistry teachers or history teachers or geography teachers for help about the area they are interested in. There should be no limit or boundary to their sources of information.

Some students may select a topic that will require an entire year's study. Others may choose one that they can complete in a matter of days. In other words, the teacher is putting the responsibility of learning upon the students' shoulders. This is something that is needed so that those students who do not go on to college nevertheless have been trained to investigate things they are interested in; they have been trained to educate themselves.

The Eclectic Methods

In this approach to learning, the teacher uses a combination of methods during the year, not one method. This has its advantage in that some students cannot respond to a given method, be it self-directed, process-managerial, or didactic. Students are not sequential, and imposing one method on them, whether it be the self-directed or the process-managerial, is just as bad as imposing the didactic. The teacher should be flexible and sensitive to the needs of his students. He can start, for example, with the lecture method and then use the process-managerial or self-directed. If the students do not respond, he can go back to lecturing.

In the Chicago school system, a science teacher changed from the lecture to the self-directed method, but the students rebelled and accused the teacher of being lazy. As a result the teacher switched back to the lecture method. This illustrates that it is better for the teacher not to structure his course and not to make it sequential so that he can remain flexible about the methods he employs during the year.

The following are some combinations of methods that could be used.

Motivated Self-Directed

In this method the teacher briefly introduces the student to the concepts of science so he can gain an appreciation of the subject. This could be done by a month or two of the lecture method, depending upon the teacher. Then the teacher might ask the class to choose an area of special interest to them which deals with the environment. The students would investigate the area they have chosen on their own, with the teacher serving as a resource person or supervisor in the class. The students select the content of the materials to be investigated. This approach is a combination of the lecture and self-directed methods.

Using a combination of methods such as the didactic and the self-directed has the advantage of reaching more students. The objectives should be to attract student attention to the problems of the community. The teacher might provide a list of possible topics if some students failed to choose their own.

29

Techniques of Learning

Make a list of some techniques you would employ in using the motivated self-directed method. Also list some possible topics pertaining to environmental science you would suggest to your students.

Process-Managerial and Self-Directed

In this method the teacher spends part of the year with the process-managerial method described earlier in this chapter. If he notices that a student is interested in working on an individual project, he lets him investigate it in depth. Or he might ask a student to indicate an area he is interested in investigating on his own, and the self-directed method can be applied here. This is one way that the curriculums advocated by the science curriculum reform movement can be used along with the self-directed method with the teachers opening their classes to the students' interests and to their study of the environment in their community.

Using this method requires careful planning by the teacher, otherwise it can be a disaster. The teacher must study the situation carefully and consult his principal. He will probably find the principal more agreeable to using this method than the self-directed approach.

Outline your plans for learning a class unit in your subject area that you would want your students to follow in investigating the environment and collecting data from their community. Indicate the procedures you would follow, and the method of evaluation you would use.

Didactic and Process-Managerial

In this approach the teacher lectures part of the year, perhaps a month or two or possibly half of the year. The rest of the time he can use the process-managerial approach described earlier in this chapter, because the students now can think for themselves and design their own procedures for reaching the objectives set forth for them by the teacher. The students have more flexibility in class, and the emphasis is on the interdisciplinary approach. The teacher still has a structured course and the student, though given a certain amount of freedom, does not select the content of the course he is taking. Some students, therefore, may not respond favorably to this method, which is not used widely. Again, it requires careful planning by the teacher. Team learning can be used in this method and in the two methods described above. A teacher may be very successful with the self-directed method and a failure with the lecture method. This may be the case with a teacher who uses the process-managerial, but fails to use the self-directed, or a teacher who is good in lecturing but not in using the process-managerial. Teachers' talents could be used here in team learning to investigate environmental problems of the community and in focusing student attention on these problems.

List the techniques you would follow in organizing a team learning unit to use the talents of the teachers in your school in studying the environmental problems of the community. Outline also the evaluation techniques you would employ for this unit.

Teaching by Contract

In this method, the student signs a contract with the teacher to perform certain tasks in order to receive the grade he wants. This method, which is finding its way into secondary schools, can be used along with the didactic, the self-directed, or the process-managerial. In the didactic method, the teacher can use this for additional assignments. For example, in addition to the grade a student will get on exams, he will be required to write papers or investigations on specific topics. If he performs them satisfactorily, he will get a grade he would like in addition to his grade on the exams. This procedure can be used with the process-managerial method where the student can work on a special project to improve his grade.

The format of the contract might be something like this:

I_____agree to perform the following task to complete Unit I.

1. Select a topic for investigation.

2. Collect my data and field observation.

3. Present my findings to the class and to the teacher.

If I violate these conditions, I understand that I will not receive the grade for which I signed this contract.

Signed,

_____

Student

_____   _____
Teacher   Date

It is to be emphasized that this format is a general one and it will vary depending on the course objectives and general conditions. This method can be used to cover one unit of independent study, or it can be used in other ways as indicated earlier. This method of learning can be helpful to students who are worried about receiving a low grade or who would like to get a better grade than what they think they will get. On the other hand, the student should be discouraged from working just for a grade.

Do you think there are any benefits in this method of learning? Make a list of the advantages and disadvantages as you see them. Try to justify each item you list.

Identify a learning unit of your choice (for example: recycling, noise in your city, etc.), then outline its objectives, topics, and learning situation. Now design a contract for the learning unit you identified.

Application and Use of Audiovisual Equipment

The introduction of television into the schools as an instructional medium was in the late 1950s. Television promised to help solve the teacher shortage, but as time progressed it was clear that TV did not solve the problem. The disadvantage of using TV as an instructional medium is that it limits communication between teacher and student. Having students jammed into large lecture halls is not the best way to help students learn.

Most of the units learned by television employ the didactic approach, so the slow learner loses interest in the subject matter. Nor does the use of television in the schools serve the purpose of getting students involved in learning about their environment and in relating to their community.

The teacher should familiarize himself with the audiovisual devices available in his school. New equipment is developed every week, and schools put heavy emphasis on the use of audiovisual equipment such as overhead and front projectors, overhead transparencies, slides, film loops, and film strips. These materials should be made available to the student as well, so that if the class is being taught by the process-managerial or self-directed method, he has access to them. The student should be trained in the proper use of the equipment so it will last a long time.

In using these audiovisual materials, the teacher should outline the objectives of the class unit and encourage students to bring slides such as those taken on vacation.

Films available in environmental science will be selected in such a way that they present data to the students without telling them everything or pointing out all that they need to know about a certain aspect of the environment. After presenting the data, the teacher can stop the projector and pose questions to the students, challenging them to come up with possible solutions. The use of audiovisual equipment should not be taken as an easy way out of learning. Instead, class lessons should be organized around the films.

The teacher also should use films that present the subject matter in an inquiry approach. Unfortunately, not many such films are available. Sometimes a film should be shown without the sound, encouraging the student to think for himself.

Students should be encouraged to use the overhead projector to report their findings, to make drawings, and to relate their data to subjects they are investigating. They should also be encouraged to make their own films about their school or their city, pointing out the environmental problems and suggesting possible solutions. Such films can serve as a school project and could be shown in a local theatre.

Before showing a film to the class, the teacher should review it so he can stop the film from time to time and generate some discussion. The teacher should also prompt some discussion to arouse the student's curiosity before showing the film.

Students should be encouraged to collect as many films or slides as possible and keep them in the resource center in the school. Sometimes resource people who have traveled extensively and who have taken films and slides can be invited to show their pictures and tell about their travels.

Can you think of any investigations in which students can make their own observations and record them with the help of audiovisual equipment? List some activities in which students could collect data. One example would be to have them record changes in the school yard or in the city.

Field Trips

One of the most effective ways of making students aware of the problems of their environment is to take them into the field, taking every precaution against their possible injury. In some cases, parents might be invited to go along. In planning a field trip, first go into the field to investigate ways in which the student can get a better look at his community and such natural processes as erosion, weathering, and pollution. After that, survey the possibilities of taking the students to certain areas to study rivers, mines, construction projects, archeological excavations, parks, museums, industrial plants, and even local offices dealing with air and water pollution.

It is a MUST for the teacher to visit the site to be studied before taking students there. He also must devote considerable time to planning the objectives, types of data to collect, etc. Several field trips to industrial plants, museums, and such end in failure due to improper planning.

Each trip should have a different objective. In visiting an office, the objective would be to ask questions and collect data. On a field trip in geology, earth science, or biology, the students should not be told what each plant, animal, geological formation, or type of cloud is. Instead, they should be told to collect their own data for later discussion. In other words, field trips should not use the didactic approach; they should be based on inquiry. The art of observation should be emphasized. In some cases, it might be wise to take students to the same area a second time to see if they can observe more things than they did the first time. If possible, the teacher should plan a field trip once a month. Sometimes, community resource people can be used, especially naturalists or other persons with the community and the surrounding areas used for field trips.

Students should be equipped with such things as hammers, plastic bags, notebooks, and cameras. And, of course, they should wear clothing suitable for a field trip.

After surveying the natural setting and resources available in your community or city, outline nine field trips that you would like your class to take during the year. Keep in mind the objectives, the techniques of getting students to understand the problems involved in each field trip, and the methods of presenting the data they collect in the field. Remember that environmental science is an interdisciplinary subject and is not limited to one given area.

The teacher knows his school and his students better than anyone else does. What applies to one class in a given school may not apply in another, but whatever the school, students should be encouraged to express their interests, needs, and ideas. It is beyond the scope of this book to outline detailed investigations for each of the sciences and the social studies, but the teacher is urged not to use the didactic method. If he has no choice, reference should be made to the available science textbooks, which offer structured investigations in great detail. For use of other methods, the teacher should refer to the first part of this chapter.

Suggestions for Student or Class Investigations

Students can investigate one or several of the following in their community.

1. Water cycle
   Precipitation
   Clouds
   Snowfall
   Evaporation
   Effect of air pollution on precipitation
   Dynamics of atmosphere

2. Rock cycle
    Weathering
    Erosion
    Transportation of sediments
    Types of rocks present and their history
    Mountain building
    Crustal movement
    Volcanism
    Geology of ocean floor
    Trenches
    Geosynclines
    Resources of the oceans

3. Food chain

4. Change

5. Air and water pollution

6. Water laws

7. Plants
    Soils
    Water budget
    History of the community
    Industry
    Mineral resources
    Trends in population growth
    Sanitary conditions

8. Waste

9. Hazard conditions

10. Social trends

11. Man and the social order

12. Ecosystems in the community

13. Efforts of industry to combat pollution

14. Recycling of resources

15. Film covering environmental problems in the community

16. Resource materials available through the community, state, regional, and national agencies. Most important is the community. A list of these materials should be made available to all students.

Suggestions for School Projects

1. Investigate what industry is doing to combat pollution

2. Allot one day a week to talk about environmental problems

3. Initiate adult education courses in environmental science

4. Investigate natural resources in the community

5. Investigate sources of pollution in the community

6. Sponsor a science fair to conserve environment in the community

7. Sponsor a lecture series on methods of solving environmental problems

8. Allot one day a month for removal of litter from the streets

9. Cooperate with other city schools to set up monitor control stations for air and water pollution

10. Stress environmental problems in the community throughout the curriculum

11. Conduct comprehensive study in the community in the following areas:

    Renewable Resources
        Air
        Wildlife
        Water
        Plants
        Forests

    Nonrenewable Resources
        Minerals
        Fossil fuel

    Human Resources
        Recreation
        Community, regional, state, and national resources
        Manpower

12. Study the history of the community's population density. Refer to the appendixes for resource materials pertaining to this chapter.

4

Suggested
Investigations

Environmental lessons should be interdisciplinary and should be designed to use the students' immediate environment throughout the year. Otherwise, students may lose interest after completing one or two investigations. They should discover the impact of science on their daily lives and the interrelationship of science and social studies. Local environmental problems should serve only as a starting point for understanding environmental problems, because if students learn only what is in their immediate environment, their education will be limited if they transfer to another school. A student living in Illinois, for example, is not likely to get excited about sea water intrusion, and discussing it would be meaningless because he hasn't come in touch with this problem. Through investigating the water resources in his community, however, the student's attention can be directed toward sea water intrusion or he may discover it for himself.

Teachers are urged to experiment and to use the self-directed approach in environmental science, giving students the thrill of discovering what science is all about. In conducting environmental investigations through the self-directed method, the teacher will be kept busy serving as a resource person. This may mean keeping track of thirty or more students in a class, but after the first few lessons, the students will have learned to depend on themselves and will not need the teacher so often.

The teacher must play an important role in directing students to investigate environmental problems. What do you think this role should be? Outline the teacher's responsibilities in conducting environmental science lessons using the self-directed approach.

Suggested Investigations

The teacher must provide a classroom environment conducive to learning by providing the following:

1. Better trust between him and the students.
2. Willingness to change his attitude to learning.
3. Willingness to accept students' ideas and to exchange ideas with students.
4. Willingness to learn with students and not to act as an authoritarian in the class.
5. Ample reference material suggesting ways for students to look up the information to complete their investigations.
6. Audiovisual equipment such as films, filmstrips, slides, transparencies, and others.
7. List of school and community resources.
8. Bulletin boards, magazines, newspapers, newsletters, and journals.

Following are some investigations in which you can involve your students, as your school permits. Each of these investigations can be dealt with by a small group of students, with each group later reporting to the class and having a general discussion. Students should be encouraged to select an area they are interested in within each investigation and to report findings, methods of procedures, and conclusions.

Water Supply

To get students to investigate the water supply in their community, the teacher can pose the following questions:

1. What is the source of the school's water supply?
2. How does this water relate to the city's water?
3. Where does the city water come from?
4. What is the source of rainwater in the city?
5. What happens to the water when it falls on the city's surface?
6. How many gallons of water does the school use monthly?
7. How many gallons of water does the city use monthly?
8. Does the city have sufficient water for its entire population? Does it have a reservoir of water? If so, how long will it last?
9. How does the water reach your school? How does it reach your home?
10. Estimate how many gallons of water you use daily.
11. Ask your school how much it pays each month for water. Can you think of ways to reduce the use of water in your school?

The ugly scene along a bank of Lake Minnetonka, north of Minneapolis, Minnesota, showing dead and dying algae which prohibits any life in these waters. This overgrown algae feeds off nutrients poured into the lake from cesspools, sewage treatment plants, and land used for agricultural purposes. Just as the algae receives excessive nutrients, so too does it grow excessively, devouring oxygen instead of giving it, until it dies and, for lack of oxygen in the water, causes the death of aquatic plants and animals (Courtesy of the Environmental Protection Agency, Washington, D.C.).

Suggested Investigations

12. Ask your parents how much they pay for water each month. Can you think of ways in which they can reduce their use of water?
13. Is the water supply constant in your city?
14. Determine how water is distributed to the city.
15. What do you think happens to the water after it is used? Where does it all end up?
16. Find out who is the number one user of water in your city. Estimate how much water is being used annually by industry, agriculture, and homes.
17. What are some of the legal problems involved in the use of surface water, such as lakes and streams, and subsurface water?

As a teacher you can stress students' findings and their effect on the students' daily lives. You can make the assignment less structured by suggesting that the class investigate the occurrence and the movement of water in your city. The class then can develop its own outline, and students can investigate various aspects of their city's water resources. The class period can be used to discuss students findings, and for interacting with each other.

For a student to carry out these investigations, he must draw on his knowledge of mathematics, physics, chemistry, biology, etc. This gives the teacher a good opportunity to stress the fundamentals of each of these sciences, their applications, and their interaction.

Sources of Water Pollution

In order to discuss the sources of water pollution in your city, you can ask students to consider the following questions:

1. What is water pollution?
2. What are the city, state, and federal standards for domestic use of water?
3. Determine whether industry contributes to water pollution. This can be done by checking the waste disposal of an industry and determining whether it ends up in major lakes or rivers in your city.
4. Determine the sources of water pollution in your town. One may be the use of fertilizers by farmers; another, leakage in the sewer system.
5. Does water pollution affect the people in your city? If so, how? Students may begin by checking with hospital records to determine how many people were hospitalized because of water pollution.

6. Does water pollution affect the economy of your city? If so, how?
7. Suggest ways of combatting water pollution in your city.
8. Does your city's water pollution affect its food chain or its ecology? If so, how?

To make their findings known, students should be encouraged to consult the major or the local newspaper.

Haverhill, Mass. A drainage pipe, or outfall, empties municipal and industrial filth, largely untreated, into the Little River, a tributary of the Merrimack River, one of New England's greatest pollution problems (Courtesy of the Environmental Protection Agency, Washington, D.C.).

Sources of Air Pollution

Before suggesting projects on air pollution, you can have a class discussion on the structure and dynamics of the atmosphere, emphasizing how an understanding of the atmosphere can help reduce air pollution. The air is composed of 78 percent nitrogen, 21 percent oxygen, .94 percent argon, .02 percent neon, and .04 percent others. Most air pollution occurs in the lower part of the stratosphere, but, because of supersonic airplanes, there also is some pollution in the ozone layer.

Instruments to detect air pollution located in various parts of Chicago (Courtesy of the Department of Environmental Control, City of Chicago).

The entire class can investigate the sources of air pollution. Here are some suggested activities for the students:

1. What does air pollution mean to you? What does it mean to the people in your city?
2. Classify the types of air pollution in your city.
3. Investigate the sources of air pollution in your city.
4. Investigate the effect of air pollution on health.
5. Investigate the effect of air pollution on buildings, cars, statues, and tombstones.
6. Single out the main source of air pollution in your city and suggest ways to combat it.
7. Investigate the effect of air pollution on your city's economy.

Burning waste may contribute to air pollution in large cities (Courtesy of the Department of Environmental Control, City of Chicago).

Are You a Polluter?

In your daily life at home and at school, you contribute to pollution. To solve environmental problems, every citizen must cooperate instead of leaving it to the state or federal government to find a solution. Many students think they can do nothing about environmental problems.

Suggested Investigations

A suggested topic for students could be to investigate themselves as polluters. They might be asked to keep a record of their daily activities at home and at school as the basis for a class discussion along these lines:

1. How does your pollution affect the economy of your city?
2. Suggest ways to reduce your pollution to a minimum.
3. How does your pollution affect your family and your classmates?
4. Determine how much money you could save by reducing your pollution.
5. Determine whether you are contributing to global pollution and suggest ways to reduce it.
6. Can you use the natural resources without pollution?
7. How does your pollution affect the ecology of your community?
8. Set up rules for yourself to reduce pollution and follow them.
9. If you doubled your pollution, how would it affect the economy of your town and your school? How would it affect the ecology of your town and the global environment?

Population

One of the principal causes of environmental problems is the population explosion. More people require more natural resources, more cars, more household equipment, more water, more of everything. Several investigations can be suggested to students. Some are:

1. Investigate the population growth in your town. Federal statistics indicate that a baby is born every nine seconds, and that someone dies every 16.5 seconds. Does this hold true in your town?
2. Investigate the principal causes of population growth in your town. Is it due to religious beliefs, poor education, or what?
3. Does your city need a plan for reducing population? If so, can you suggest one?
4. Investigate your city's population growth during the last fifty years. Do you see any trends? What causes these trends?
5. If population growth tripled in your town, how would this affect its economy and ecology?
6. Does your city's pollution affect its population growth? If so, how?
7. Is your city doing anything about its population growth? Is it doing enough? If not, why not?
8. Investigate the methods used to control population growth in your city.

9. Investigate the attitudes of a selected sampling of people in your city toward population growth.
10. Trace your own family's growth as far back as possible and suggest ways in which it affected the lives of your relatives in the past, and how it is affecting you today.
11. Survey studies which have been conducted concerning anatomical, physiological, and behavioral changes in humans and in other animals resulting from, or related to, changes in population density.

Chicago Riverbank cleanup (Courtesy of the Department of Environmental Control, City of Chicago).

Trace the History of Your Town

Throughout America's history, cities have been built and have disappeared while others are still around. It would be an exciting project for students to familiarize themselves with city growth and to learn how the structure of the city functions.

Here are some investigations that can be suggested to students:

1. Trace the history of your city since it was founded.
2. Investigate its natural resources.
3. Investigate the structure of its governing body.

4. Investigate its projected growth.
5. Investigate why people leave your city.
6. If you were to construct the city in which you live, how would it differ from the way it was originally built?
7. Investigate your city's actions and policies to combat pollution. Are they enough? Can you suggest ways to improve them?
8. Investigate the presence of industrial and commercial companies in your city. Are they there because of the geographic location, the presence of natural resources, or some other reason?
9. Investigate the contributions your city is making to the state, the country, and the world.
10. Investigate ways in which you can make your city unique and a better place to live.

Chicago Riverbank cleanup (Courtesy of the Department of Environmental Control, City of Chicago).

Do You Know Your Town?

It is essential for both the teacher and the student to become familiar with the town in which they live so the student may gain a better appreciation of his environment. The following activities can be suggested to students at the beginning of the year:

1. Take a tour of your city, or a part of it if it is large, and record what you see. Take another tour a week or a month later and again record what you see. Compare both lists. How do they differ? Suggest ways of making yourself more observant.
2. Investigate the resources in and outside your school.
3. Investigate the ecology of your town. Is there any relationship between its components? Is one dependent on the other? How?
4. Is your town changing? If so, how? Define the change and suggest ways to observe it.
5. Investigate the types of plants in your town. Suggest ways to classify them.
6. Investigate the types of ethnic groups in your town and the reason for their presence.
7. Investigate ways in which you can improve the appearance of your town.
8. Investigate the drug problem in your town. Suggest ways to combat it and conduct a survey to get some reaction to this problem.
9. Write a poem or an essay describing your town.

Recycling

Recycling is one of the most effective ways of combatting environmental pollution, especially when our natural resources are being rapidly depleted. Recycling investigations can offer a challenge to students, especially in large cities. Here are some suggested activities:

1. Investigate the garbage sites in your town and determine the amount of garbage dumped daily.
2. Investigate your town's treatment of garbage. For example, is it burned, buried, or used again?
3. Investigate how many bottles the people in your town use. What percentage are returnable bottles? What happens to the bottles after they are used? Are they being recycled?
4. Investigate the annual use of paper in your town. How much of it is recycled?
5. Investigate a garbage site and list the things that are in the garbage. Determine how many of them can be recycled.
6. Investigate how much money your town can save by recycling paper and bottles.

Suggested Investigations

7. Investigate how much money your school can save by recycling paper, bottles, and cans.
8. Investigate the reactions of townspeople to recycling. Report your findings to your class and to the city council.
9. Investigate the effect of garbage and waste disposal on the ecology of your city.
10. Plot the locations of garbage and waste disposal and determine whether they contribute to pollution. For example, are they located near the river? Does water falling on the surface permeate the garbage to the subsurface water? Is human and industrial waste being recycled in your town? If it is, what effect does it have on the economy of your town? If not, find out why it is not and determine the advantages of recycling this waste.

The Oceans

The oceans constitute 75 percent of the earth's surface, and with our natural resources being depleted, man is paying more attention to the resources of the ocean. But there may not be enough of them by the time he needs these resources. An understanding of the oceans will help students gain a better understanding of the environmental problems facing them now and in the future.

Here are some suggested activities:

1. Investigate the history of the oceans since their birth.
2. Investigate an ocean close to you and list ways in which it affects your daily life.
3. Investigate the benefits of exploring the oceans.
4. Investigate the sources of pollution in the oceans. Classify them and suggest ways of combatting the pollution.
5. Investigate whether pollution of the oceans affects you and your town.
6. Investigate the effect of pollution on life in the oceans.
7. Investigate the possibility of living on the ocean floor. Is it feasible? Do you think man can live safely on the ocean floor and be self-supporting?
8. Investigate the natural resources of the oceans. Are you using any of them in school or in your town? Classify these resources.
9. Investigate the role oceans play in the water and rock cycles.
10. Write an essay or a poem about man's use and misuse of ocean resources through history.

Energy

Energy plays an important part in the processes that have been active in and on the earth. Without energy man could not exist. An understanding of the source and transfer of energy therefore is essential. Here are some suggested ways of involving your students in the study of energy:

1. Investigate sources and types of energy in your town.
2. Investigate whether energy does transfer in and outside of your town.
3. Construct cycles for energy used in your town.
4. Suggest ways of consuming energy in your town.
5. Investigate the availability of energy in your town and suggest ways of providing energy if your town's population were doubled.
6. Investigate the relationship of energy to pollution in your town. For example, does energy contribute to pollution? If so, how?
7. Investigate the flow of energy in light of the processes that occur in your town.
8. Write a poem or an essay on the role energy plays in your town.
9. Determine whether you waste energy. If so, can you suggest ways to reduce the waste?
10. Suggest a new source of energy in your town. Discuss the feasibility of its use.

Portable Sound Level Meter (Courtesy of B&K Instruments, Inc., Cleveland, Ohio).

Suggested Investigations

Noise Pollution

Noise pollution is harmful to the human body, so it is essential for students to realize at an early age that noise pollution can have harmful effects on their bodies for the rest of their lives. To familiarize students with noise pollution, here are some suggested investigations:

1. Ask students to define what noise pollution means to them.
2. Ask them to classify noise pollution in their town.
3. Ask them to determine what contributes the most noise in their town and to suggest ways to prevent it.
4. Ask students to determine how many people in their town are affected by noise pollution; that is, how many lose their hearing and are affected in other ways.
5. Ask them to investigate how noise pollution affects them economically. The loss of hearing, for example, will affect their work and their chances for advancement.
6. Ask students to investigate how noise pollution is measured and the instruments used.
7. Ask them to investigate the noise pollution laws in their town. If the town has none, ask the students to suggest some.
8. Ask students to investigate whether they contribute to noise pollution and to suggest ways of reducing it.
9. Ask them to write a poem or an essay describing what noise pollution is and how they can reduce it because of its harmful effects on the townspeople.
10. Ask students to investigate people who have lost their hearing to determine how they lost it and how its loss affected them.

Investigating Your Town's Transportation System

Transportation systems are essential for moving people and goods, and for the advancement and existence of cities. In order to help your students understand the transportation system in your town, suggest the following investigations:

1. Ask students to draw a map showing your town's transportation system.
2. Ask them to classify the system.
3. Ask students to trace the history of transportation systems and to learn how they have varied through time.
4. Ask them to suggest ways of improving your town's transportation system.
5. Ask them to investigate ways in which transportation systems can be made safer.

50

6. Ask students to investigate how the transportation system was built.
7. Ask them how the transportation system affects their town's economy.
8. Ask students to investigate ways of reducing accidents on streets and highways.
9. Ask them to write a poem or an essay stressing the need for highway safety.
10. Ask them to investigate ways in which they personally can improve their town's transportation system.

Nuclear Pollution

The sharp increase in population and the demand for energy have encouraged industry to construct nuclear power plants at a rapid pace, although their safety has not yet been proven. Look at figure 2 and see whether a nuclear plant has been built or is being built in your state. Nuclear pollution is disastrous to mankind because it affects not just one city but the entire population of our planet. Nuclear pollution will be one of the principal topics of discussion during this decade, so it is essential for students to become aware of it. Here are some suggested investigations to give them that awareness:

1. Investigate the type of power your city uses to generate electricity.
2. Investigate the advantages and disadvantages of constructing a nuclear power plant in your town.
3. Investigate the safety precautions necessary to generate a nuclear power plant.
4. Investigate the reactions of your city's residents to constructing such a plant.
5. Investigate the impact of a nuclear power plant on the economy of your town.
6. Suggest possible alternatives to the use of nuclear power as a major source of energy.
7. Investigate whether your city is a suitable site for a nuclear power plant.
8. Write an essay or a poem describing the dangers of nuclear pollution.
9. Suggest ways in which your class can make the residents of your city aware of nuclear pollution.
10. Investigate the difference between natural and nuclear radiation and their impact on you and your city.

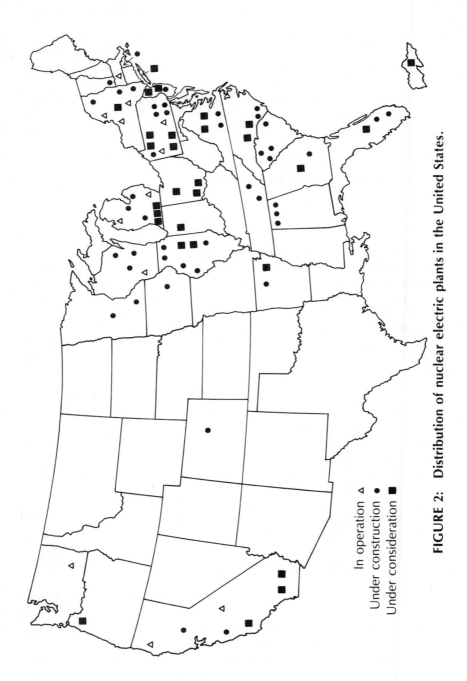

FIGURE 2: Distribution of nuclear electric plants in the United States.

In operation △
Under construction ●
Under consideration ■

Natural Hazards

Earthquakes, erupting volcanoes, landslides, soil erosion, movement of rock strata, and flooding of streams and rivers are natural hazards that occur frequently, and the student is likely at some time to come in touch with one of them in his town. Therefore, it is essential for him to become aware of these hazards. Here are some suggested investigations for students to make in their town:

1. Investigate the natural hazards that have occurred in your town during the last fifty years.
2. Investigate the laws of your town concerning safety precautions to protect the buildings against natural hazards.
3. Investigate soil erosion in your town and suggest ways to prevent it.
4. Investigate the economic effects of natural hazards on your town.
5. Suggest ways in which you can inform residents of your city so that they may prepare for natural hazards.
6. Investigate the causes of natural hazards.
7. How do natural hazards affect the ecology of your city?
8. Investigate how residents of your city unconsciously contribute to conditions that cause natural hazards.
9. Investigate the effect of natural hazards on your town's population growth.
10. Write an essay or a poem about natural hazards and their effect on the growth of your town.

Food Chain

Plants are dependent on sun, water and soil; animals are dependent on plants and on each other. Man depends on both for his existence. It is essential for students to understand the interplay and the dependence of plants and animals on each other so they can better appreciate and conserve their environment. Here are some investigations you can use:

1. Investigate the type of plants and animals in your city.
2. Prepare a diagram showing their interrelationship and interdependence.
3. Select one plant and investigate how its extinction because of pollution can affect the entire food chain. Do the same kind of investigation about an animal.
4. Investigate the chemicals your city uses to eliminate certain plants or insects.
5. Investigate the effect of these sprayed chemicals on the food chain of animals.

Tornadoes—like this one—are most apt to be wholesale killers when they are least expected. Contrary to popular opinion, tornadoes can—and do—strike in all fifty states of the nation. It is the citizen's responsibility to know the tornado safety rules and to keep a "tornado watch" if so advised by the National Weather Service of the National Oceanic and Atmospheric Administration (NOAA) in the U.S. Department of Commerce (Courtesy of NOAA).

Soil erosion can be minimized by constructing terraces, diversions, and by using contour strip cropping (U.S.D.A.—Soil Conservation Service).

6. Investigate the laws in your city concerning hunting, spraying of chemicals, and removal of plants.
7. Suggest ways in which you can inform the residents of your city about the dangers of upsetting the food chain.
8. Select a plant and an animal. Investigate how eliminating them would affect the city's economy.
9. Write a poem or an essay stressing the danger of upsetting the food chain.
10. Investigate your food chain.

Investigating Polluted Water

Lakes and rivers are becoming polluted because man insists on using them as a dumping ground. To stress the difference between polluted and clean water, such as tap and distilled water, you can suggest that the class do the following:

1. Investigate the water's color.
   a. Causes.
   b. Source.
   c. Pollution potential.
2. Investigate the water's odor.
   a. Classify it.
   b. Determine source.
   c. Determine its effect on health.

Suggested Investigations

3. Investigate the turbidity of lake or river water.
   a. Obtain samples from different locations.
   b. Obtain samples from different depths.
4. Investigate the difference between acidity or alkalinity of lake and tap or distilled water.
   a. Which is more acidic?
   b. What makes it more acidic?
5. Investigate their salinity.
   a. Which is more saline?
   b. What causes this salinity?
   c. How does salinity differ from acidity?
6. Suggest a way to detect the presence of silica, aluminum, and iron oxides in your samples.
      Investigate their source.
7. Investigate the effect of your findings (1-6) on people's health in your town.
   a. Which chemical is most dangerous to health?
   b. How many people became sick because of the water?
8. Investigate the effect of your findings (1-7) on the economy of your town.
   a. How much will it cost your town to remove pollution?
   b. Is this pollution affecting your town's recreational areas?

Investigating Carbon Dioxide in Water

Carbon dioxide, which is water soluble, is considered harmful to fish. An increase of carbon dioxide in the air increases the dissolved amount of carbon dioxide in water. The free gas reacts with water to form carbonic acid. Both carbonic acid and the free gas are toxic to fish life. Carbonic acid has a dissolving action on building materials.

To make your students aware of carbon dioxide in their environment, here are some suggested activities:

1. Investigate the amount of free and reacted carbon dioxide. Carry out the measurement with:
   a. Samples of water from different river locations.
   b. A sample of freshly boiled water.
   c. Tap water.
   d. Sewage water.

Discuss the above findings.

2. Discuss the effect of temperature on the carbon dioxide content of a sample.

56

3. Investigate the effect of carbon dioxide on fish.
   a. Bubble carbon dioxide into a fish aquarium for five minutes a day for three weeks.
   b. Compare the results to an aquarium where carbon dioxide was not bubbled.
4. Investigate the effect of carbon dioxide on the ecology of a lake or a river in your town.
5. Investigate the effect of water into which carbon dioxide is being constantly bubbled on a piece of cement.
   a. Measure loss of weight in the cement.
   b. Repeat using tap water.
   c. Repeat using water in which sulfur dioxide has been added.
6. Investigate the effect of your findings (1-5) on the economy of your city.

Investigating Phosphate Pollution

Phosphates are among the major lake and river pollutants. A test for the presence of phosphate in your water might be interesting. Refer to a quantitative analysis textbook to determine phosphate content in:

1. Tap water.
   a. Distilled water.
   b. River or lake water.
   c. Sewage from a sewage plant.
   d. Solutions of different kinds of detergents.

Comment on your findings.

2. Investigate the effect of various concentrations of phosphates on fish in an aquarium.
3. Investigate the laws in your city or state concerning the use of phosphates (example: detergents).
4. Investigate the effect phosphates have on human health.
5. Investigate the effect of phosphates on the ecology of your city.
6. Suggest ways of informing your city's residents of the dangers to their environment in the use of phosphates.
7. Write an essay, a poem, or a song describing the direct effect of phosphates on the economy of your city.

Investigating Sulphur Dioxide Pollution

Increased use of coal and oil contributes to the increase of sulphur dioxide in the air. In several cities, this has proved to be a hazard to human

Suggested Investigations

health and to vegetation. Advances in petroleum and petrochemical industries have produced further amounts of sulphur dioxide. Here are some suggested activities for your students:

1. Investigate the presence of SO_2 in the gas coming out of a car exhaust. For example: Hold a ⏝ tube containing a solution of iodine and potassium iodide close to the exhaust. Back titration of the remaining iodine by a standard thiosulphate gives a measure of SO_2 or H_2S evolved.
2. Repeat the above investigation by bubbling a small sample of air into your standard solution. Do you find a strong evidence of sulphur dioxide? Suggest explanations.
3. Examine the effect of sulphur dioxide on marine life, e.g., bubbling sulphur dioxide into an aquarium. Compare with a standard.
4. Examine the effect of sulphur dioxide on vegetation by bubbling it into a small greenhouse. Compare with a standard.
5. Investigate the laws in your city to prevent sulphur dioxide pollution.
6. Investigate the effect of sulphur dioxide on the economy of your town.
7. Investigate what effect sulphur dioxide pollution has had on the health of your city's residents.
8. Write an essay or poem stressing the effect of sulphur dioxide on ecology, buildings, cars, and human health in your city.
9. Investigate the amount of sulphur dioxide released into your city's air by cars (one gallon of gasoline produces 0.13 ounce of sulphur dioxide).
    Determine how many gallons of gasoline are sold daily in your city.

Investigating Mercury Pollution

Mercury is now being used in many processes in industry, and the escape of appreciable amounts of mercury into the environment is responsible for fetal poisoning. Your students may be engaged in some activities such as these:

1. Explore which industries use mercury. Why do they use it?
2. Estimate how much mercury is being used daily. What measures are being taken to minimize its escape into the environment?
3. Suggest ways to minimize the use of mercury and other ways to minimize its escape in your city.

4. Try to determine the number of cases in which mercury poisoning was fatal, the number in which it was not.
5. Suggest a test for detection of mercury pollution. Try it out on a sample of:
    a. Lake or river water.
    b. Soil.
    c. Food, e.g., tuna.
6. Investigate the laws in your city concerning mercury pollution.
7. Suggest ways to inform the townspeople about the harmful effects of mercury pollution.

Refer to the appendixes for resource material pertaining to this chapter.

5

Student
Evaluation

Evaluation may be defined as a plan to secure evidence that learning took place, whether formal or informal. Educators have long been searching for effective methods of evaluating learning. In European and Asian countries, and even in the United States, there is a lack of evaluation methods to assess the success of pre-college and college education.

Since 1951, the federal government has supported twenty-five curriculums to improve social and science programs in elementary and secondary schools at a cost of $85,391,069. For all these programs, there was no effective plan for evaluating their success, and in one case a program was dropped and another initiated because the first program was not evaluated and its success was limited to only a few schools. In funding these programs, the National Science Foundation has not provided money for evaluating their success.

Evaluation is essential to the success of any program because it provides information on its weaknesses and strengths. Evaluation data do not necessarily solve problems but they provide some insight into programs. The type of data collected is important because it determines what is to take place in a given program. The methods teachers use therefore definitely affect the future learning of students, as reported in a study by Joseph Gehrman, who found that students' ability to better their achievements has definitely been affected by their teachers' evaluation methods.

Do you recall how you were evaluated in your secondary school and in the college courses you have taken so far? Outline methods of evaluation that you experienced in high school and college and suggest ways of improving evaluation in high school.

Student Evaluation

Evaluation should be a lifelong process. It does not end with finishing one unit or even one class, yet teachers usually evaluate only one aspect of learning. Few high schools follow up on their students to determine their success in life after graduation as a gauge of the effectiveness of their programs.

Teachers use such traditional techniques as a card file record of a student's performance on exams, quizzes, and oral quizzes. Thus the student is judged as to his ability, his standing in class, and his performance as compared to the national norms.

To develop an evaluation program, several points need to be considered:

1. The behavioral objectives and skills outlined for the program and for evaluation should be made clear.
2. The methods and criteria of evaluation should be outlined.
3. The school's facilities and the student's environment should be part of the evaluation.
4. Parents should play an important role in helping to evaluate student learning. This has largely been ignored in the past.
5. Evidence of changes in a student's attitudes should be recorded and considered as part of the evaluation program.
6. The methods of learning should be evaluated bearing in mind that students usually learn only what they are going to be examined on.
7. Methods of collecting data should be outlined and made clear.
8. Students should participate in the evaluation program. They should be interviewed and even serve on the evaluation panel.
9. The evaluation findings should be incorporated in the curriculum in order to improve it. All major unsolved problems or anticipated problems should be considered but should not be overemphasized.
10. Teachers should be evaluated every year, and their innovations in learning and contributions to make their classes attractive to all levels of students must be considered. Students should be allowed to evaluate their teachers.

Can you think of some uses for evaluation? Make an outline of some of them.

Students generally concentrate on what is expected of them and make judgments about what they have learned. Teachers, on the other hand, use evaluation to assess their effectiveness; they compare a student's performance with their objectives for a given course. Parents use the evaluation data to assess the success of the curriculum as reflected in their children's achievements. School administrators use the same information to assess their schools' effectiveness in preparing students for a better life.

Grades often are used as a threat, with teachers disregarding how students learn. Instead of designing evaluation models that best fit their schools, teachers use the same methods they experienced when they were in college, or they use standardized tests that are not always the most effective evaluation tools. Standardized tests are widely used in the secondary schools. Such tests have advantages and disadvantages. Make a list of the advantages and disadvantages that you think of for standardized tests.

Some advantages for using standardized exams are as follows:

1. Teachers will have less work because they won't have to prepare for exams.
2. The standardized exams created by experts in the field are designed to evaluate the objectives of each particular course.
3. They provide an efficient way of assessing national curriculums.

Here are the disadvantages:

1. A standardized exam does not really tell what a student knows about the subject matter. He will not be tested on much of what he has learned.
2. The exams are not relevant to all geographic areas.
3. A standardized exam makes the student answer using somebody else's words. He does not have an opportunity to use his own vocabulary.

There are no standardized exams as yet in environmental science, because environmental science is an interdisciplinary subject and because the environment varies from town to town. The student environment also varies.

There are several major unsolved evaluation problems:

1. None of the evaluation techniques developed so far includes collecting data about the learner and the learning process.
2. Evaluation models have been inflexible because objectives were inflexible. Thus, evaluation was restricted because objectives were restricted.

    Knowledge of how students learn is extremely important in evaluation, yet it is something teachers are not asked to evaluate. Evaluation models also lack continuity in evaluating a student's progress from year to year.
3. Such progress should be kept up to date in order to evaluate whether the student has applied the knowledge gained from his classes. Sometimes a student underrated in a given class does

much better in a later class because he has learned more than what the teacher has evaluated him on.

ITEM   STUDENT NAMES

Questions conclusions
Interacts with other students
Asks questions
Thinks critically and contributes to class discussion
Works to his ability
Works willingly with groups
Hands in assignments on time
Disturbs class
Interrupts class discussion
Can relate to other areas in science and social studies
Can interrelate to other areas in science and social studies
Can work on his own
Is able to collect and interpret data
Uses library rarely—often—everyday
Does not waste time in class
Shows respect for others
Considers other ideas willingly
Remains flexible in his conclusions as evidence is gathered
Uses laboratory equipment with care
Makes an educated guess
Has a keen sense of observation
Is doing well in other science classes
Shares his data with other class members
Shows interest in other projects
Recognizes unsolved problems
Reports his findings clearly
Others

TABLE 1.   Checklist for evaluating students in an environmental education class.

Assume that you are helping students learn environmental science or environmental education. What evaluation method would you use? Develop a model for evaluating students in an environmental education class.

Since environmental science is an interdisciplinary subject, it will include areas from other disciplines, such as the sciences and the social studies. Develop an evaluation model that will include other faculty members (grades 7-12).

Assume that you want to do away with exams and quizzes. What method would you use? Several teachers have found the checklist effective because they can evaluate students on more than what they score on a test. Prepare your own checklist for evaluating your students.

Table 1 is a checklist you might find useful in your class. It can be modified to fit your classroom needs.

Each teacher should be encouraged to develop his own method of evaluating students, since facilities vary from school to school and the environment varies from town to town or from one part of town to another. But in learning environmental science or environmental education in secondary schools, it is essential for the teacher to develop a method that recognizes the interdisciplinary aspect. Table 2 refers to a model for comparison of the student and teacher evaluation in the didactic approach. You will notice that in this model the evaluation is terminated by the teacher, while the student evaluation is continued because the student can evaluate himself best. He will know whether he understood material assigned by the teacher. This method is not provided for in any evaluation model available today.

For further information on the application of the three domains (psychomotor, cognitive, and affective domain), you may refer to *Behavioral Objectives and Evaluational Measures: Science and Mathematics* by Robert Sund and Anthony Picard, Charles E. Merrill, 1972.

Assume that you are helping students to learn about environmental science and are asked to develop a model for evaluating your students using the didactic approach. After examining the model explained in table 2, suggest ways to improve evaluation. One suggestion, for example, would be to ask the student to submit multiple questions, essay questions, or true-false questions. Then select the best questions asked by the students. Or you can ask the students to make the tests and grade them on that, because in order to make a test they will have to master the material studied.

If you are to use the process-managerial approach in environmental education, what method would you use to improve evaluation in your class? Refer to table 3, which compares the teacher evaluation and the student evaluation.

In the process-managerial approach, evaluation is limited to the objectives set by the teacher, but what if the student selects his own content? What procedures would be used for evaluation? Develop a model for evaluating students in the self-directed method.

TEACHER   STUDENT

outlines his objectives   outlines his objectives

                                 evidence of learning reflected on

evidence of expected outcome

                                 (Teacher Evaluates)
                                 Exams
Card   Reports
Exams   Quizzes
Reports   Laboratory
Quizzes   Oral?
Laboratory
Oral?

                                 Teacher Does Not Evaluate
                                 a. Whether students apply what they learn in
                                    other classes.
Evaluation   b. Whether students apply what they learn in
                                    their community.
        is   c. Whether students make future use of
                                    knowledge gained.
terminated.

                                 Evaluation is

                                 continuous

                                 by the students.

**TABLE 2. Model of student and teacher
evaluation in didactic approach.**

TEACHER	STUDENT
Outlines objectives and selects content	Selects what he wants to learn
	Develops his own procedure
Suggests procedure	Reacts only to what the teacher asks
Discusses according to objectives	
Tests according to objectives	Masters only what is on exam
	Other learning took place but is unmeasured by the teacher.

TABLE 3. Comparison of teacher and student evaluation in the process-managerial method.

Most evaluation techniques on methods of learning described in available textbooks employ some of Bloom's taxonomy on behavioral objectives.[1] Such techniques are useful for structured methods of learning. Refer to them and suggest ways to restructure them for use in an environmental science class.

In using the self-directed approach, students often ask about the grading procedure because they are accustomed to a system in which they are graded by an exam. Students should be asked to suggest ways of assessing their grades (table 4). After all, they are the ones investigating a given area and they can best evaluate themselves. Here, the teacher will have to trust the student, eliminating differences between them.

If you still wish to evaluate students yourself, here are some suggestions:

1. Ask students to outline any number of unsolved problems they have found in the areas they investigated.
2. Ask students to design their own exam, then give it to them. This could be done individually.
3. Ask students to select and discuss in depth a topic other than the one they investigated.
4. Ask students to discuss the area they investigated in relation to other areas and concepts in environmental science.
5. Ask students to write ten or fifteen multiple choice questions. To do so, students will need considerable information, and the questions they submit will give you an idea of the extent of their study.
6. Ask students to submit ten references they have used, so you can judge how deeply they studied their subject matter.

---

1. Benjamin S. Bloom, *Taxonomy of Educational Objectives* (New York: David McKay Company, 1956).

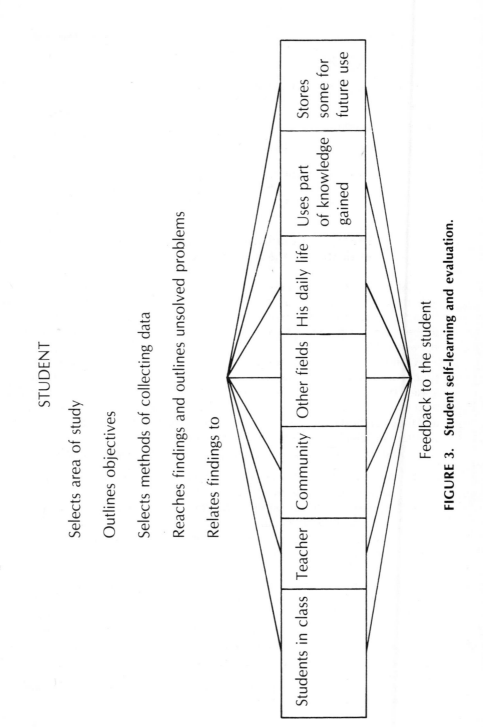

STUDENT

Selects area of study

Outlines objectives

Selects methods of collecting data

Reaches findings and outlines unsolved problems

Relates findings to

| Students in class | Teacher | Community | Other fields | His daily life | Uses part of knowledge gained | Stores some for future use |

Feedback to the student

FIGURE 3. Student self-learning and evaluation.

If you are using learning by contract, use various methods unless you are using only the lecture or process-managerial approach with minor additional assignments.

In chapter three you developed a contract evaluation procedure. Revise your procedure where necessary, based on information about evaluation you have obtained since that time.

Some Tips on Evaluation

1. At the beginning of the year, ask students to suggest the best way to evaluate them and assess their grades for the course.
2. Ask each student to hand in five questions about each unit covered. Eliminate repetitious questions and use the rest as the test.
3. As often as possible, use open book exams.
4. Avoid memory or recall questions.
5. Use learning by contract as often as possible so you can eliminate the threat between you and the students.
6. Allow students to grade themselves and ask them to justify their grades in one written paragraph.
7. Evaluate students on all daily aspects of school activities. Evaluation should be comprehensive, not limited to one class. An evaluation of reading, for example, should include all aspects of reading, not just that of reading novels. History, science, and even mathematics should also be evaluated even though little reading is required.
8. Emphasize methods of obtaining and analyzing data, not just how to get the correct answer.
9. Allow students to take tests when they feel like it. They should not be required to take a test on a day when they are not feeling well.
10. Wherever possible, follow up on the progress or performance of your students in other science classes. This will require the cooperation of other faculty members.
11. Involve parents in evaluation because they can be a very effective tool. Teachers should keep parents constantly informed about their children's progress not just by sending reports on grades but by feedback information.

BIBLIOGRAPHY
Atkin, J. M. "Behavioral Objectives in Curriculum Design: A Cautionary Note." *The Science Teacher* 35 (May 1968):27-30.

Broadhurst, A. N. "An Item Analysis of the Watson-Glaser Critical Thinking." *Science Education* 54, no. 2 (April–June 1970).

Cook, L. D. "Management Control Theory as the Context for Educational Evaluation." *Journal of Research and Development in Education* 3, no. 4 (Summer 1970).

Dancy, L. T. "Evaluating the On-Going Public School Program." *Journal of Research and Development in Education* 3, no. 4 (Summer 1970).

Student Evaluation

Fischler, A. S., and Zimmer, George. "The Development of an Observational Instrument for Science Teaching." *Journal of Research in Science Teaching* 5, no. 2 (1967–68).

Flanders, Ned A. *Interaction Analysis in the Classroom: A Manual for Observers.* rev. ed. Ann Arbor: School of Education, University of Michigan, 1964.

_____. "Interaction Analysis: A Technique for Quantifying Teacher Influence," in Edmund J. Amidon and John B. Hough, eds., *Interaction Analysis: Theory, Research and Application* (Reading, Mass: Addison-Wesley, 1967) pp. 3-15.

_____. *Interaction Analysis in the Classroom.* Ann Arbor: School of Education, University of Michigan, 1966.

Forehand, G. A. "Curriculum Evaluation as Decision-Making Progress." *Journal of Research and Development in Education* 3, no. 4 (Summer 1970).

Gehrman, J. L. *A Study of the Impact of Authoritative Communication of Expected Achievement Upon Actual Achievement in Elementary School Science.* Doctor Dissertation Abstracts, 26 November 1959, pp. 2559-60.

Kresh, E. "Evaluation in a Multi-Level Agency." *Journal of Research and Development in Education* 3, no. 4 (Summer 1970).

Kuhn, D. I. "Behavioral Objectives in the Life Sciences: A Useful Instrument in Curriculum Development." *Science Education* 54, no. 2 (April–June 1970).

Lindsay, B. R. "A Unified Approach to Science Teaching." *Journal of Research in Science Teaching* 5, no. 3 (1970).

Lundin, G. E., and Welty, Gordon A. "Management Models and Educational Evaluation." *Journal of Research and Development in Education* 3, no. 4 (Summer 1970).

Merriman, O. H. "From Evaluation Theory into Practice." *Journal of Research and Development in Education* 3, no. 4 (Summer 1970).

Provus, M. "Evaluation for Decision-Making, Choice and Value." *Journal of Research and Development in Education* 3, no. 4 (Summer 1970).

Raun, C. E., and Butts, David. "The Relationship Between the Strategies of Inquiry in Science and Student Cognitive and Effective Behavioral Change." *Journal of Research in Science Teaching* 5, no. 33 (1967–68).

Raun, C. E., and McGlathery, Glenn E. "Elementary School Science Methods: One View and One Approach." *Science Education* 54, no. 3 (September–July 1970).

Saadeh, I. "The Teacher and the Development of Critical Thinking." *Journal of Research and Development in Education* 3, no. 1 (Fall 1969).

Suchman, J. R. *Evaluating Inquiry in Physical Science.* Science Research Associates, 1969.

Torgerson, K. J., and Engel, Dorothy. "Individualized Science with Behavioral Objectives." *The Science Teacher,* November 1970.

Walbesser, H. H. *An Evaluation Model and Its Application,* Second Report Commission on Science Education of the American Association for the Advancement of Science. Washington, D.C., 1968.

Watson, F. G. "Research on Teaching Science." *Handbook of Research on Teaching.* New York: Rand-McNally, 1963.

Van Deventer, W. C. "Evaluating Students Understanding of Ideas in Junior High School Science." *The Science Teacher,* November 1970.

Appendix
A

Sources of Information

Books, Booklets, and Articles

Agricultural Research Service. *Safe Use of Pesticides—In the Home—In the Garden.* Washington, D.C.

American Cancer Society. *Biology Experiments for High School Students.* (Obtain from local branches.)

American Chemical Society. *Cleaning Our Environment—A Chemical Basis for Action.* Washington, D.C., 1969.

American Petroleum Institute. *Conservation.* New York, 1970.

Anthrop, Donald F. "Environmental Noise Pollution: A New Threat to Sanity." *Bulletin of the Atomic Scientists,* May 1969.

_____. "Applying Concepts About Air to the Study of Atmospheric Pollution." *Science,* Junior High School Edition. Advance Planning Issue 1970–1971. New London, Conn.: Croft Educational Services, pp. 5-8.

Atomic Energy Commission. *New Developments in Radioactive Waste Management.* Washington, D.C.: Government Printing Office, 1969.

Bear, Firman E. *Earth: The Stuff of Life.* Norman: University of Oklahoma Press, 1962.

Berelson, Bernard. "Beyond Family Planning." *Science* 163, no. 3867 (February 1969):533-43.

Bergstrom, George. *Too Many: A Study of Earth's Biological Limitations.* New York: Macmillan, 1969.

Appendix A

Bjormson, Bayard F.; Pratt, Harry D; and Littig, Kent S. *Control of Domestic Rats and Mice*. Washington, D.C.: Government Printing Office, 1969.

Boolootian, Richard A., and Thomas, June. *Marine Biology*. New York: Holt, Rinehart & Winston, 1967.

Brehman, Thomas, and Qutub, Musa. "Environmental Activities and Problem Solving." *The Science Teacher* 38, no. 4 (April 1971):55-56.

———. "Survival City Project. An Environmental Awareness Project." *The Science Teacher* 38, no. 3 (October 1971):72.

Bresler, Jack B. *Environments of Man*. Reading, Mass.: Addison-Wesley, 1968.

Carr, Donald E. *Death of Sweet Waters*. New York: W. W. Norton, 1966.

Carter, Luther J. "DDT, the Critics Attempt to Ban its Use in Wisconsin." *Science* 163, no. 3867 (February 7, 1969):548-51.

———. "The Population Crisis: Rising Concern at Home." *Science* 166, no. 3906 (November 7, 1969):722-26.

Chandler, T. J. *Fresh Water*. Garden City, N.Y.: Doubleday, 1969.

———. *The Air Around Us*. Garden City, N.Y.: Doubleday, 1969.

Chase, M. *Field Guide to Edible and Useful Wild Plants of North America*. NASCO Nature Study Aids, 1965.

Chase, M., and Chase, C. *Field Guide to Tracks of North American Wildlife*. NASCO Nature Study Aids, 1970.

Chiapetta, Jerry. "Great Lakes—Great Mess." *Audubon,* May/June, 1968.

Citizen's Committee For Clean Water. *Citizen Action for Clean Water*. New York, 1965.

———. *Conservation and the Water Cycle*. Washington, D.C.: Government Printing Office.

———. *Control of Pesticide Residues in Foods: Industry Guidelines*. Washington, D.C.: Government Printing Office.

Cook, Robert C., and Becht, Jane. *People: An Introduction to the Study of Population*. Washington, D.C.: Columbia Books, 1968.

Crocker, T. D. "Some Economics of Air Pollution Control." *Natural Resources Journal* 8-2, April 1968.

Curtis, Richard, and Hogan, Elizabeth. *Perils of the Peaceful Atom*. New York: Ballantine Books, 1970.

Davis, Robert K. *The Range of Choice in Water Management: A Study of Dissolved Oxygen in the Potomac Estuary*. Baltimore, Md.: Johns Hopkins Press, 1968.

DeBeck, Paul. *Biological Control of Insect Pests and Weeds.* New York: Reinhold, 1964.

DeBell, G., ed. *The Environmental Handbook.* New York: Ballantine Books, 1970.

Ecotactics. New York: Pocket Books, 1970.

Ehrlich, Paul R. *The Population Bomb.* New York: Ballantine Books, 1968.

Eisenbud, Merril. *Environmental Radioactivity.* New York: McGraw-Hill, 1963.

"Expanding Educational Opportunities for Disadvantaged Youth." *Outdoor Education.* Oakland, Md.: Garrett County Science Center, 1967.

Federal Program in Population Research. Parts one and two of Report to Federal Council for Science and Technology, Washington, D.C., 1969.

Graham, Frank Jr. *Since Silent Spring.* Boston, Mass: Houghton Mifflin, 1970.

Gries, Mary Louise. *Experiences of the World in Plants.* Chicago: Jewel Industries, 1965.

Gross, M. Grant. *Oceanography.* Columbus, O.: Charles E. Merrill, 1967.

Hardin, Garrett, ed. *Science, Conflict and Society.* San Francisco: W. H. Freeman, 1969.

_____. *Population, Evolution and Birth Control, A Collage of Controversial Ideas.* San Francisco: W. H. Freeman, 1964.

Heimler, Charles, and Lockard, J. David. *Focus on Life Science.* Columbus, O.: Charles E. Merrill, 1969.

Herber, Lewis. *Crisis in Our Cities.* Englewood Cliffs, N.J.: Prentice-Hall, 1965.

Hersh, Seymour M. *Chemical and Biological Warfare: America's Hidden Arsenal.* New York: Anchor, 1968.

Hunter, Donald C., and Wohlers, Henry C., eds. *Air Pollution Experiments for Junior and Senior High School Science Classes.* Pittsburgh, Pa.: Air Pollution Control Association, 1969.

_____. *Air Pollution Experiments for High School.* Pittsburgh, Pa.: Air Pollution Control Association, 1968.

Izaak Walton League of America. *Citizen Guide to Action for Clean Water.* Glenview, Ill., 1966.

Jarrett, Henry, ed. *Environmental Quality in a Growing Economy.* Baltimore, Md.: Johns Hopkins Press, 1966.

Kastner, Jacob. *The Natural Radiation Environment.* Oak Ridge, Tenn.: AEC Division of Technical Information, 1968.

Klingebiel, A. M. *Know the Soil You Build On.* Washington, D.C.: Government Printing Office, 1967, p. 13.

Appendix A

Knipling, Edward. "Alternate Method of Controlling Insect Pests." *FDA Papers* 3, no. 1, 1969, p. 24.

Landsberg, Hans H. *Natural Resources for U.S. Growth—A Look Ahead to the Year 2000.* Baltimore, Md.: The Johns Hopkins Press for Resources for the Future, Inc., 1965, p. 260.

Landsberge, Halmut E. *Weather and Health: An Introduction to Biometeorology.* Garden City, N.Y.: Science Study Series, Anchor Books, Doubleday, 1969, p. 148.

League of Woman Voters. *Consideration of Federal Financial Incentives to Industry for Abating Water Pollution.* 1200 17th St., N.W., Washington, D.C., 1966, p. 20.

_____. *So You'd Like to Do Something about Water Pollution.* 1200 17th St., N.W., Washington, D.C., 1969.

_____. *Who Pays for a Clean Stream?* 1200 17th St., N.W., Washington, D.C., 1966.

_____. *Population+Production=Pollution.* 1200 17th St., N.W., Washington, D.C., 1965.

_____. *Land and Water for Tomorrow—Training Community Leaders.* 1200 17th St., N.W., Washington, D.C., p. 44.

Lieber, Leslie. *The Battle of Bugs.* Washington, D.C., *Sunday Star,* 21 September 1969, pp. 4-5.

McKinney, R. E. "The Environmental Challenge of Solid Waste." *Technology Review* 70, no. 7 (May 1968):35-39.

McElroy, William D. "Biomedical Aspects of Population Control." *Bioscience* 19, no. 1 (January 1969):19-23.

Mesthene, Emmanuel G. *Technological Change—Its Impact on Man and Society.* Cambridge, Mass.: Harvard University Press, 1970.

Milne, Lorus, and Milne, Margery. *The Balance of Nature.* New York: Alfred Knopf, 1960.

Moss, Frank E. *The Water Crisis.* New York, Washington, London: Fredrick A. Praeger, 1967.

National Academy of Science. *The Growth of U.S. Population.* Washington, D.C., 1965.

_____. *Waste Management and Control—A Report to the Federal Council of Science and Technology.* National Research Council, 1966, p. 257.

National Association of Countries. *Community Action Program for Water Pollution Control.* 1001 Connecticut Ave., N.W.,Washington, D.C., 1967, p. 182.

Navarra, John G. *Our Noisy World.* Garden City, N.Y.: Doubleday, 1969.

Neal, Charles D., and Perkins, Otho E. *Science Skilltexts.* Columbus, O.: Charles E. Merrill, 1966.

Nearing, Scott, and Nearing, Helen. *Living the Good Life.* Social Science Institute. New York: Schocken Books, 1970.

Nelson, D. J., and Francis, C. E. *Symposium on Radiocology, Proceedings of the Second National Symposium, Ann Arbor, Michigan,* 1967. Springfield, Va.: Clearinghouse for Federal Scientific and Technical Information, National Bureau of Standards, U.S. Department of Commerce, p. 774.

Norris, Kenneth S. "The Third Fish." *New Republic,* 9 May 1970.

_____. *Observing Our Environment Through Our Five Major Senses—See, Feel, Hear, Smell and Taste.* Davenport, Iowa: Handicapped Children's Nature Study Center, 1970.

Office of Economic Opportunity. *Need for Subsidized Family Planning Services: U.S. Each State and County.* Washington, D.C.: Government Printing Office, 1968.

Office of Science and Technology. *Considerations Affecting Steam Power Plant Site Selection.* Washington, D.C.: Government Printing Office.

Perloff, Harvey S. *The Quality of the Urban Environment.* Baltimore, Md.: The Johns Hopkins Press for Resources for the Future, Inc., 1969.

Planned Parenthood. *1969 Publications About Planned Parenthood.* New York.

_____. *A Selected Bibliography: Family Planning, Population, Related Subjects.* New York.

Popkin, Roy. *Desalination: Water for the World's Future.* New York: Fredrick A. Praeger, 1968, p. 235.

Population Crisis Committee. *Reports of the Victor Fund for the International Planned Parenthood Federation.* Washington, D.C.

Population Reference Bureau. *Population Bulletin.* Washington, D.C.

_____. *Population Bulletin: A Sourcebook on Population* XXV, no. 5 (November 1969).

President's Science Advisory Committee. *Report on Use of Pesticides.* Washington, D.C.: Government Printing Office, 1963.

_____. *Proceedings of the Conference on Noise as a Public Health Hazard.* Washington, D.C.: American Speech and Hearing Association, 1968.

Qutub, Musa. "Environmental Science Bibliography." *Mid-Continent Scientific,* September 1971.

Appendix A

Qutub, Musa. "Make Earth Science Relevant." *Science Activities,* October 1971, pp. 28-32.

Rainwater, Lee. *And the Poor Get Children.* Chicago: Quadrangle Books, 1967.

Ramey, J. T. *Licensing and Environmental Considerations in Atomic Power Development.* Washington, D.C.: Division of Public Information.

_____. *Report of the United Nations' Scientific Committee on Effects of Atomic Radiation.* United Nations, General Assembly, 17th session, suppl. 16, 1962.

Rudd, Robert L. *Pesticides and the Living Landscape.* Madison: University of Wisconsin Press, 1964.

Science Teacher. Special issue on environmental education, April 1970.

_____. Special issue on conservation, April 1967.

Seaborg, G. T. *Science, Technology and the Citizen.* Washington, D.C.: Atomic Energy Commission, Division of Public Information, 1969.

Shuttlesworth, Dorothy E. *Clean Air—Sparkling Water.* Garden City, N.Y.: Doubleday, 1968.

Sladen, Brenda K., and Bang, Frederick B. *Biology of Populations.* New York: American Elsevier Publishing Co., 1969.

Soil Conservation Society of America. *Making Rural and Urban Land Use Decisions.* Ankeny, Iowa, p. 40.

Soleri, P. *Ecology: The City in the Image of Man.* Scottsdale, Ariz.: The Cosanti Foundation.

Stewart, George R. *Not So Rich as You Think.* New York: Houghton Mifflin, 1968.

Strong, A. L. *Open Space for Urban America.* Washington, D.C.: Government Printing Office.

_____. *The Right To Exist—A Report on Our Endangered Wildlife.* Washington, D.C.: Government Printing Office, p. 12.

_____. *Terrestrial Ecology.* Washington, D.C.: Government Printing Office, 1967.

_____. *Facts for Consumers: Pesticide Residues.* Department of Health, Education and Welfare. Washington, D.C.: Government Printing Office, 1964, p. 12.

_____. *Fish, Wildlife and Pesticide.* Department of the Interior, Fish and Wildlife Service. Washington, D.C.: Government Printing Office, 1966, p. 12.

_____. *Interagency Environmental Hazards Coordination Pesticides and Public Policy.* Subcommittee on Reorganization and International Organizations, Committee on Governmental Operations. Washington, D.C.: Government Printing Office, 1966.

_____. *Disposal of Liquid Wastes by Injection Underground Neither Myth Nor Millennium.* U.S. Geological Survey Circular 631. Washington, D.C.: Government Printing Office, 1969, p. 15.

_____. *Drinking Water Standards.* Department of Health, Education and Welfare. Washington, D.C.: Government Printing Office, 1962, p. 61.

_____. *Water Pollution Aspects of Urban Runoff.* Washington, D.C.: Government Printing Office, 1969, p. 272.

_____. *What is Water?* Washington, D.C.: Government Printing Office, 1967.

_____. *What You Can Do About Water Pollution.* Washington, D.C.: Government Printing Office, 1968.

_____. *The Migration of Birds.* Department of the Interior, Fish and Wildlife Service. Washington, D.C.: Government Printing Office, 1962, p. 8.

_____. *Water Quality Standards.* Washington, D.C.: Government Printing Office, 1969.

_____. *National Wildlife Refuges.* Department of the Interior, Fish and Wildlife Service. Washington, D.C.: Government Printing Office, 1968, p. 14.

_____. *Restoring Surface Mined Lands.* Washington, D.C.: Government Printing Office.

_____. *Know Your Soil.* Agri-Info Bulletin No. 267. Washington, D.C.: Government Printing Office, 1963.

_____. *Soil Conservation Districts: What They Are, How They Work, How SCS Helps Them.* Washington, D.C.: Government Printing Office, 1968.

_____. *What is a Watershed?* Washington, D.C.: Government Printing Office, 1969.

_____. *Man and Nature in the City: A Symposium to Explore the Role of Nature in the Urban Environment.* Department of the Interior. Washington, D.C.: Government Printing Office.

_____. *Soil, Water, and Suburbs.* Washington, D.C.: Government Printing Office, 1968.

_____. *The Why and How of Rural Zoning.* U.S. Department of Agriculture. Washington, D.C.: Government Printing Office, 1967, p. 58.

_____. *The Creek and the City.* Department of the Interior. Washington, D.C.: Government Printing Office, 1967.

_____. *Sediment—It's Filling Harbors, Lakes and Roadside Ditches.* Washington, D.C.: Government Printing Office, 1967.

_____. *Slowdown: For Water.* Washington, D.C.: Government Printing Office, 1966.

Appendix A

Strong, A. L. *Suggested State Water Pollution Control Revised.* Washington, D.C.: Government Printing Office, 1966.

_____. *Snow Surveys.* Washington, D.C.: Government Printing Office, 1965.

_____. *Water and Industry.* Washington, D.C.: Government Printing Office, 1962.

_____. *Water Facts: Sources, Supply, Needs, Uses, Losses, Floods, Conservation.* Department of Agriculture. Washington, D.C.: Government Printing Office, 1964.

_____. *Water for Cities—The Outlook.* Washington, D.C.: Government Printing Office, 1969.

_____. *Estuaries—Cradles of Graves.* Department of the Interior, Federal Water Pollution Control Administration. Washington, D.C.: Government Printing Office, 1967.

_____. *Federal Water Pollution Control Act.* Department of the Interior, Federal Water Pollution Administration. Washington, D.C.: Government Printing Office, 1967.

_____. *Movement of a Solute in the Potomac River Estuary at Washington, D.C. at Low Inflow Conditions.* Geological Survey Circular 529-B. Washington, D.C.: Government Printing Office, 1969.

_____. *The Northeast Water Supply Crisis of the 1960's.* Washington, D.C.: Government Printing Office, 1968.

_____. *Pollution Caused Fish Kills 1968.* Washington, D.C.: Government Printing Office, 1968.

_____. *Quantitative Comparison of Some Aesthetic Factors Among Rivers.* U.S. Geological Survey Circular 620. Washington, D.C.: Government Printing Office, 1969.

_____. *Pesticides.* Washington, D.C.: Government Printing Office.

_____. *Study of Pesticides in Shellfish and Estuarine Areas of Louisiana.* Public Health Service. Publ. No. 999-UIH-2. Washington, D.C.: Government Printing Office, 1967.

_____. *From Sea to Shining Sea.* The Presidents Council on Recreation and Natural Beauty. Washington, D.C.: Government Printing Office, 1968.

Terrill, J. G., Jr.; Haward, E. D.; and Legget, I. Paul, Jr. "Environmental Aspects of Nuclear and Conventional Power Plant." *Industrial Medicine and Surgery* 36, no. 6 (July 1967):412-19.

U.S., Atomic Energy Commission. *The Nuclear Industry, 1969.* Washington, D.C.: Government Printing Office.

78

_____. *Nuclear Power: Benefits and Risks.* Washington, D.C.: Government Printing Office, 1969.

_____. *Annual Report to Congress,* 1968. Washington, D.C.: Government Printing Office, 1968.

U.S., Atomic Energy Commission and U.S., Department of Health, Education and Welfare. *Partners in Protection: Joint Federal—State Radiation Control.* Washington, D.C.: Government Printing Office.

U.S., Department of Agriculture. *Our Struggle Against Pests.* Washington, D.C.: Government Printing Office.

U.S., Department of Commerce. *Current Population Reports: Population Estimates and Projections.* Washington, D.C.: Government Printing Office.

U.S., Department of Health, Education and Welfare. *Biological Effects of Radiation.* Washington, D.C.: Government Printing Office.

_____. *Radiological Health Data and Reports.* Washington, D.C.: Government Printing Office.

U.S., Department of the Interior. *The Practice of Water Pollution Biology.* Federal Water Pollution Control Administration. Washington, D.C.: Government Printing Office.

_____. Geological Survey. *Water Resources Investigations In California.* Washington, D.C.: Government Printing Office, 1969.

_____. *A Report—Population and Family Planning The Transition from Concern to Action.* Washington, D.C.: Government Printing Office.

Water Pollution Control Administration. *Focus on Clean Water.* Washington, D.C.: Government Printing Office, 1966.

Water Resources Council. *Alternative Institutional Arrangements for Managing Basin Operations.* Washington, D.C.: Government Printing Office, 1967.

Whitten, Jamie L. *That We May Live.* New York: D. Van Nostrand, 1966.

Whyte, W. H. *Cluster Development.* American Conservation Association. New York, 1964.

Wilson, D. G. "Technology and the Solid Waste Problem." *Technology Review* 71, no. 4 (February 1969):20-33.

Young Women's Christian Association. *Community Action for Conservation and Outdoor Recreation.* New York, 1965.

Magazines

American Education Publications. *Current Science.* Science Division, 55 High St., Middletown, Conn. 06457

American Institute of Architects. *American Institute of Architects.* 1735 New York Ave., N.W., Washington, D.C.

American Museum of Natural History. *Natural History.* Central Park West at 79th St., New York, N.Y. 10024

American Society of Agronomy. *Agronomy Journal.* 677 S. Sego Rd., Madison, Wis.

American Society of Landscape Architects. *Landscape Architecture.* 344 Peterson Ave., Louisville, Ky. 40205

Architectural Design. 26 Bloomsbury Way, London, W.C. 1.

Buttenheim Publishing Corporation. *American City.* 757 Third Ave., New York, N.Y.

Congressional Quarterly, Inc. *Congressional Quarterly.* 1735 K St., N.W., Washington, D.C. 20006

Conservation Foundation. *The Conservation Foundation Letter.* 1250 Connecticut Ave., N.W., Washington, D.C. 20036

Defenders of Wildlife. *Defenders of Wildlife News.* 731 Dupont Circle Bldg., Connecticut Ave., Washington, D.C.

Dembar Educational Research Services, Inc. *Environmental Education.* Box 1605, Madison, Wis.

Environment. 438 N. Skinker Blvd., St. Louis, Mo.

Environmental Action. 2000 P St., N.W., Washington, D.C. 20036

Food and Drug Administration. *FDA Papers.* 200 C. St., Washington, D.C. 20204

Fortune. 540 North Michigan Avenue., Chicago, Ill.

Freed Publishing Company. *Land Pollution Reporter.* P. O. Box 1144 FDR Station, New York, N.Y.

National Association of Home Builders. *Homebuilding.* 1625 L St., N.W., Washington, D.C.

National Audubon Society. *Audubon.* 1130 Fifth Ave., New York, N.Y. 10028

National Parks Association. *National Parks Magazine.* 1701 18th St., Washington, D.C.

National Science Teachers Association. *Science and Children.* 1201 16th St., N.W., Washington, D.C. 20036

National Science Teachers Association. *The Science Teacher.* 1201 16th St., N.W., Washington, D.C. 20036

National Wildlife Federation. *National Wildlife Magazine.* 534 N. Broadway, Milwaukee, Wis. 53202

_____. *Ranger Rick's Nature Magazine.* 534 N. Broadway, Milwaukee, Wis. 53202

Natural History Society. *Naturalist.* Medical Arts Bldg., Minneapolis, Minn.

New Scientist. 128 Long Avenue, London, W.C. 2

Pacific Search, Journal of Natural Science in the Pacific Northwest. 200 Second Ave., N., Seattle, Wash.

Science. 1515 Massachusetts Ave., N.W., Washington, D.C. 20005

Science Activities Magazine. 8150 Central Park, Skokie, Ill.

Sierra Club, Inc. *Sierra Club Bulletin.* 1050 Mills Tower, San Francisco, Calif. 94104

Soil Conservation Society of America. *Soil and Water Conservation Journal.* 7515 N. East Ankeny Rd., Ankeny, Iowa. 50021

State of New York Conservation Department. *The Conservationist.* Albany, N.Y.

The Whole Earth Catalog. 558 Santa Cruz, Menlo Park, Calif.

Urban America. *Architectural Forum.* 111 W. 57th St. N.W., New York, N.Y. 10022

Urban America. *City.* 1717 Mass. Ave., N.W., Washington, D.C.

Films

American Petroleum Institute. *To Clear the Air.* New York, N.Y.

Conservation Foundation. *For All to Enjoy.* 1250 Connecticut Ave., N.W., Washington, D.C. 20036

Coronet Films and Filmstrips. *Communities Depend on Each Other.* Chicago, Ill.

_____. *Our Community Utilities.* Chicago, Ill.

Ealing Corporation. *A Volcano in Action.* Cambridge, Mass.

_____. *Flash Flood.* Cambridge, Mass.

_____. *Geographic Causes of Deserts.* Cambridge, Mass.

_____. *Habitats.* Cambridge, Mass.

Appendix A

Ealing Corporation. *The Changing City.* Cambridge, Mass.

———. *The Underseas World of Jacques Cousteau.* Cambridge, Mass.

Keep America Beautiful Films. *Heritage of Splendor.* New York, N.Y.

U.S. Government Printing Office. *Catalog of Free Films on Air Pollution.* Washington, D.C. Descriptions of the following films are given:
A Day at the Dump.
A Matter of Attitudes.
Air of Disaster.
Air Pollution and YOU.
Air Pollution in the New York-New Jersey Interstate Area.
Air Pollution: Take a Deep, Deadly Breath.
Beware of Ill Winds.
Beware the Wind.
Don't Leave it All to the Experts.
Ill Winds on a Sunny Day.
It's the Only Air We've Got.
On a Clear Day You Can Almost See Terminal Tower.
Pollution.
Something in the Wind.
The Poisoned Air.
The Run-Around.
This Business of Air.
With Each Breath.

Appendix

B

Addresses of Governmental and Other Related Agencies

Air Pollution Control Association
Publications
4400 Fifth Ave.
Pittsburgh, Pa. 15213

American Cancer Society
219 E. 42nd St.
New York, N.Y. 10017

American Conservation Association
30 Rockefeller Plaza
New York, N.Y. 10020

American Forest Institute
Education Division
1835 K St., N.W.
Washington, D.C.

American Forestry Association
919 17th St., N.W.
Washington, D.C.

American Petroleum Institute
School Program
1271 Avenue of the Americas
New York, N.Y. 10003

Basic Books, Inc.
404 Park Ave., South
New York, N.Y. 10016

Board of Education, New York City
Bureau of Curriculum Development
131 Livingston St.
Brooklyn, N.Y. 11201

Bureau of Mines and Geology
University of Idaho
Moscow, Idaho

Bureau of Outdoor Recreation
Department of the Interior
Division of Information
19th and C Streets, N.W.
Washington, D.C. 20240

Conservation and Environmental
    Science Center
Box 2230 R. D. 2
Brown Mills, N.J. 08025

The Conservation Foundation
1250 Connecticut Ave., N.W.
Washington, D.C. 20036

Creative Educational Society, Inc.
Product Information
515 N. Front St.
Mankato, Minn.

Appendix B

Doubleday & Company, Inc.
School and Library Division
501 Franklin Ave.
Garden City, N.Y. 11530

Federal Water Pollution Control
  Administration
Clean Water Publications
U.S. Department of the Interior
Washington, D.C. 20242

Forest Service, U.S. Department of
  Agriculture
Information and Education
Room 3223 South Agriculture Bldg.
Washington, D.C. 20250

Harcourt Brace Jovanovich, Inc.
757 Third Ave.
New York, N.Y. 10022

D. C. Heath & Company
ELHI Division
125 Spring St.
Lexington, Mass. 02173

Holt, Rinehart & Winston, Inc.
383 Madison Ave.
New York, N.Y. 10017

Houghton Mifflin Company
Educational Division
110 Tremont St.
Boston, Mass. 02107

Interstate Printers & Publishers, Inc.
Conservation Books
19 N. Jackson St.
Danville, Ill. 61832

The Johns Hopkins Press
Baltimore, Md. 21218

LaMotte Chemical Products
  Company
Educational Products Division
Chestertown, Md. 21620

Charles E. Merrill Publishing
  Company
1300 Alum Creek Drive

Columbus, Ohio 43216

Mid-Continent Scientific
5616 N. St. Louis
Chicago, Ill. 60659

National Wildlife Federation
1412 Sixteenth St., N.W.
Washington, D.C. 20036

The Nature Conservancy
1522 K St., N.W.
Washington, D.C. 20005

Oceanographic Education Center
Box 585
Falmouth, Mass. 02541

Oceanography Unlimited, Inc.
Sales and Marketing
108 Main St.
Lodi, N.J. 07644

Rand McNally & Company
Box 7600
Chicago, Ill. 60680

Resources for the Future, Inc.
1755 Massachusetts Ave., N.W.
Washington, D.C. 20036

Society of American Foresters
1010 Sixteenth St., N.W.
Washington, D.C. 20036

Soil Conservation Service of the
  U.S. Department of Agriculture
Educational Relations Department
U.S. Department of Agriculture
South Building, Room 6207
Washington, D.C. 20250

Southern Forest Institute
One Corporate Square, N.E.
Atlanta, Ga. 30329

Sport Fishing Institute
Education Division
719 13th St., N.W.
Washington, D.C. 20005

U.S. Atomic Energy Commission
Division of Technical Information
Washington, D.C. 20545
Attn: Hazel Whitaker

U.S. Department of Agriculture
Washington, D.C.

U.S. Department of Agriculture
Agricultural Research Service
Federal Center Building
Hyattsville, Md. 20782

U.S. Department of the Interior
Geological Survey
Washington, D.C. 20242

U.S. Government Printing Office
Superintendent of Documents
Washington, D.C. 20402

The Viking Press, Inc.
625 Madison Ave.
New York, N.Y. 10022

Franklin Watts, Inc.
845 3rd Ave.
New York, N.Y. 10022

Appendix
C

Selected Resource Centers*

Air Pollution

Air Pollution Control Association
4400 Fifth Avenue
Pittsburgh, Pa. 15213
Tel: 412-621-1100

Primarily concerned with the promotion of atmospheric pollution control, the improvement of air sanitation, and air purification as related to smoke, dust, and smog. Makes available professional papers, technical articles and publications, and descriptive materials pertaining to the cause, effect, and remedy of processes involving atmospheric pollution. Publishes *Journal of the Air Pollution Control Association,* monthly, and *APCA Abstracts,* monthly.

Air Pollution Control Committee
American Foundrymen's Society
Golf and Wolf Roads
Des Plaines, Ill. 60016
Tel: 312-824-0181

Has published information on air pollution in foundries and provides information and consultation as time permits.

Air Pollution Technical Information Center
National Air Pollution Control Administration
10313 Wade Street
Raleigh, N.C. 27605
Tel: 919-755-4616

Collects basic data on the chemical, physical, and biological effects of varying air quality, and other information on the prevention and control of air pollution.

---

*Obtained from the National Referral Center, Science and Technology Division, Library of Congress.

Provides either citations, abstracts, or extracts selected from its file of literature. Prepares state-of-the-art reviews.

American Industrial Hygiene Association
25711 Southfield Road
Southfield, Mich. 48075
Tel: Not listed

Answers questions and provides reference and referral services. Publishes *American Industrial Hygiene Association Journal,* monthly, and an *Air Pollution Manual.*

Bay Area Air Pollution Control District
939 Ellis Street
San Francisco, Calif. 94109
Tel: 415-771-6000

Collects and makes available technical information on air pollution. Maintains a library for reference.

Bureau of Air Pollution Control
Pennsylvania Department of Health
P.O. Box 90
Harrisburg, Pa. 17120
Tel: 717-787-6547

Provides literature on air pollution and its control on request. Maintains a pollutant inventory and provides consulting services.

Center for Air Environment Studies
Pennsylvania State University
226 Chemical Engineering II
University Park, Pa. 16802
Tel: 814-865-1415

Performs research and collects and provides information on air pollution, fumes, air pollution laws, effect of gases on plants, particles in air, and related subjects.

Committee on Air Pollution Controls
American Society of Mechanical Engineers
345 East 47th Street
New York, N.Y. 10017
Tel: 212-752-6800

Publishes information on air pollution, including a guide to research.

Committee for Environmental Information
435 North Skinker Boulevard
St. Louis, Mo. 63130
Tel: 314-863-6560

Answers questions, provides reference services and also provides advisory and consulting services in the field of air pollution and its effect on our environment. Publishes *Scientist and Citizen,* 10 times a year.

Environmental Pollution Center
Midwest Research Institute
425 Volker Boulevard
Kansas City, Mo. 64110
Tel: 816-561-0202

Answers questions and provides brief reference services free of charge. Complex services are provided on a fee or a contract basis. Has collected numerous materials on pollution of the atmosphere. Also provides referral services to other organizations and agencies concerned with air pollution.

Industrial Gas Cleaning Institute
Box 448
Rye, N.Y. 10580

Collects and provides information on air pollution, the effect of industrial gas cleaning on public health, methods, and equipment. Directs inquiries to cooperating members for consultation.

Los Angeles County Air Pollution Control District
434 South San Pedro Street
Los Angeles, Calif. 90013
Tel: 213-629-4711

Answers questions concerning the air pollution and smog problems in the Los Angeles metropolitan areas. Most reports are free. Publishes *News Report,* monthly; *Quarterly Contaminant Report;* and *Air Pollution Data for Los Angeles County,* annually.

Statewide Air Pollution Research
University of California at Riverside
Fawcett Laboratory
Riverside, Calif. 92502
Tel: 714-787-5123

Coordinates all air pollution research activities within the statewide program of the university. Provides information and referral services.

Biological Effects of Radiation

Armed Forces Radiobiology Research Institute Library
U.S. Department of Defense
Bethesda, Md. 20014
Tel: 301-295-1330

Provides information services as time permits on radiobiology; physiology; biochemistry; chemistry; pathology; immunology; psychology; dosimetry; etc. Publishes *AFRRI Scientific Reports* and *AFRRI Technical Notes.*

Biogeochemical Ecology Information Center
Oak Ridge National Laboratory
Building 2001, X-10

Appendix C

Oak Ridge, Tenn. 37830
Tel: 615-483-1410

Answers brief technical inquiries on stability and change in ecological systems to include the distribution of dry matter, elements, isotopes, and energy in ecosystems. Maintains files of tabular information on element inventories which include material on trophic levels (in plants, animals, and microorganisms), etc.

Bureau of Radiological Health
Consumer Protection & Environmental Health Service
U.S. Public Health Service
12720 Twinbrook Parkway
Rockville, Md. 20852
Tel: 301-443-3516

Provides information on the health hazards in exposure to ionizing radiation, measurement of environmental radiation levels, etc. Publishes the *Radiological Health Data and Reports,* monthly.

Department of Environmental Health
Scientific Activities Division
American Medical Association
535 North Dearborn Street
Chicago, Ill. 60610
Tel: 312-527-1500

Provides information on air and water pollution, fluoridation of public water supply, automotive safety, blood banks, communicable disease control, disaster medical care and health training in defense emergencies, and radiation and radioactivity. Services are primarily for physician members and allied health groups.

Division of Technical Information Extension
U.S. Atomic Energy Commission
P.O. Box 62
Oak Ridge, Tenn. 37831
Tel: 615-483-4352

Questions are answered free for high school students on up to researchers and manufacturers. Has published several reports of interest, e.g. *What's Available in the Atomic Energy Literature* (TID-4550), free; *Understanding the Atom Series,* 1966; and several special booklets. *Is affiliated with the information resources asterisked below.

Environmental Engineering Research Center
College of Engineering
University of Florida
Gainesville, Fla. 32601
Tel: 904-392-0834

Answers inquiries related to the Laboratory's research activities which include environmental radiation monitoring and the determination of the translocation and accumulation of specific radionuclides in ecological systems, especially those in-volved in food chains.

*Environmental Mutagen Information Center
Biology Division
Oak Ridge National Laboratory
P.O. Box Y
Oak Ridge, Tenn. 37830
Tel: 615-483-7072

Primarily concerned with every compound tested for mutagenecity due to their biological activity. Provides information on mutagenecity, teratogenecity, and cytotoxicity or the effects of chemicals on nucleic acid, chromosomes, mitotic division, meiotic division, oogenesis, and spermatogenesis.

*Information Center for Internal Exposure
Oak Ridge National Laboratory
P.O. Box X
Oak Ridge, Tenn. 37830
Tel: 615-483-1165

Performs technical calculations, supplies information, and interprets data rele-vant to dose received from internally deposited radionuclides. Primarily for AEC contractors, government agencies, and scientists or professional people concerned with estimation of dose from radioactive materials in the body.

*Information Integration Group
Lawrence Radiation Laboratory
Biomedical Division
University of California
Livermore, Calif. 94550
Tel: 415-447-1100, Ext. 8351

Primarily concerned with the implications of radionuclide releases into the bio-sphere by nuclear explosive devices, prediction of distribution within the biosphere and particularly in man subsequent to release, and the development of counter-measures. Will answer inquiries as time permits.

International Nuclear Information System
International Atomic Energy Agency
P.O. Box 590
A-1010 Vienna, Austria

Provides information on the peaceful use of atomic energy and related subjects.

Medical Betatron Project
University of Illinois College of Medicine
P.O. Box 6998
Chicago, Ill. 60680
Tel: 312-663-7291

Answers inquiries for information on radiation damage (high energy x-ray and electron beam), radiation safety, radiotherapy, and betatrons.

National Council on Radiation Protection and Measurements
4201 Connecticut Avenue, Suite 402
Washington, D.C. 20008
Tel: 202-363-6644

Answers inquiries for information on radiation, to include protection criteria and standards; maximum permissible dose equivalents for the population and radiation workers; maximum permissible concentrations of radionuclides inhaled or digested by humans; maximum permissible body burdens; relative biological effectiveness and quality factors, etc. Services are given within limited time permitted.

National Library of Medicine
8600 Rockville Pike
Bethesda, Md. 20014
Tel: 301-496-6095

Open to the public, the Library answers technical questions, assists in literature searches, and lends materials on an interlibrary loan basis. It publishes the monthly *Index Medicus,* a listing of the world periodical literature of the biomedical sciences, covering 150,000 items each year, and is available from the Superintendent of Documents, Government Printing Office, Washington, D.C. 20402. Publishes selected bibliographies on the biological effects of radiation on Man.

Noise Pollution, Science, and Technology

Acoustical Society of America
335 East 45th Street
New York, N.Y. 10017
Tel: 212-685-1940

Does not provide reference or document services but suggests cooperating members for consultation. Publishes its *Journal,* monthly, and *Sound—Its Uses and Control,* bimonthly.

Bolt, Beranek, and Newman, Inc.
50 Moulton Street
Cambridge, Mass. 02138
Tel: 617-491-1850

Conducts government and privately sponsored research in architecture, physical engineering, and psychoacoustics. Brief reference services are provided without charge. Technical consultations and extended literature searches are provided on a contract basis.

Committee for Environmental Information
438 North Skinker Boulevard
St. Louis, Mo. 63130
Tel: 314-863-6560

Answers inquiries on man's effect on the environment. Publishes *Scientist and Citizen,* 10 times a year. Permits onsite use of its collections. Provides advisory and consulting services.

Department of Highways and Traffic
Government of the District of Columbia
District Building
Washington, D.C. 20004
   Has sponsored a study on streets, highways, and traffic noise (1961) and can provide pertinent information.

Department of Occupational Health
American Medical Association
535 North Dearborn Street
Chicago, Ill. 60610
Tel: 312-527-1500, Ext. 417
   Provides multiservices primarily for physician members of the Association and allied health workers. Subject coverage includes the effects of noise pollution in industry.

The Greater London Council
County Hall
London, S.E. 1, England
   Has performed a study on traffic noise in the city and can advise on the availability of information.

Industrial Hygiene Foundation
5231 Centre Avenue
Pittsburgh, Pa. 15232
Tel: 412-682-2100
   Provides information primarily to its member companies and associations on environmental and occupational medicine. Has several publications including the *Annotated Bibliography on Noise—Its Measurement, Effects, and Control* (1955, $7.50). May have compiled listings of noise control agencies.

Institute of Environmental Stress
University of California
Santa Barbara, Calif. 93106
Tel: 805-961-2361
   Studies problems of function, organization, and adaptive potentials of human and other organisms and processes in relation to the environment and its changes. Provides assistance as time and staff permit. Has done studies on the effect of noise on humans and other organisms.

Laboratory of Psychophysics
Harvard University
33 Kirkland

Cambridge, Mass. 02138
Tel: 617-868-7600

Performs research on the effect of noise on humans. Provides consulting services primarily to sponsors, to others as time and regulations permit. Research results are published in reports and professional journals.

National Swedish Institute for Building Research
Linnegatan 64
Stockholm 0, Sweden

The Institute, in cooperation with the National Swedish Institute for Public Health, has performed research on traffic noise in dwelling areas.

Office of Noise Abatement (TST-50)
U.S. Department of Transportation
Washington, D.C. 20590
Tel: 202-426-4553

Provides information on request. Suggests additional organizations for consultation and information. Prepares reports on the effect of noise from various means of transportation.

Scientific Reference Service
Bureau of Occupational Safety and Health
U.S. Environmental Control Administration
1014 Broadway
Cincinnati, Ohio 45202
Tel: 513-684-2682

Provides brief and detailed answers to technical questions pertaining to toxicology and hazards of industrial materials and conditions; control of hazards; injurious effects on health; prevention and treatment, etc. No fees for services or materials, except for extensive literature searches.

Sound Section
Metrology Division
U.S. National Bureau of Standards
Washington, D.C. 20234
Tel: 301-921-3607

Should be able to supply reference and referral information on sound environment, noise pollution and control.

Oil Pollution

American Institute of Merchant Shipping
1120 Connecticut Avenue, N.W.
Washington, D.C. 20036
Tel: 202-833-2710

Services limited to member companies and approved individuals. Its Special Committee on Oil Pollution can provide information concerning the legal aspects of the problem. Publishes quarterly legislative reports. Materials prepared for specific use of member steamship companies, government agencies, and approved mailing lists; services to others as time and staff permits.

Library, American Petroleum Institute
1801 K Street, N.W.
Washington, D.C. 20006
Tel: 202-833-5600

Provides information on oil pollution and its control to inquirers. Has prepared studies on this subject which are available from the Institute.

Chemical Engineering Branch
Office of Merchant Marine Safety
U. S. Coast Guard
400 7th Street, S.W.
Washington, D.C. 20591
Tel: 202-526-1217

Answers questions from interested inquirers on oil pollution and control of oil slicks. Also provides referral services.

Great Lakes Commission
2200 North Campus Boulevard, #5104
Ann Arbor, Mich. 48105
Tel: 313-665-9135

Serves as clearinghouse for information on the Great Lakes and the Great Lakes Basin. Has done studies on pollution of the area by oil tankers. Publishes *Great Lakes News Letter,* six times a year; *Report to the States,* biennially; and *Great Lakes Research Checklist,* twice a year.

IDRES (Institute for the Development of Riverine and Estuarine Systems)
Information Center
Science Information Services
Franklin Institute Research Laboratories
Benjamin Franklin Parkway at 20th Street
Philadelphia, Pa. 19103
Tel: 215-448-1230

Has done studies on oil pollution of rivers and estuaries. May be able to provide results of studies or refer requesters to appropriate sources.

Institute of Microbiology
Rutgers—The State University
University Heights Campus, Hoe Lane
New Brunswick, N.J. 08903

The Institute performs research on the biodegradation of oil slicks under contract to the Office of Naval Research. It provides information in accordance with regulations.

Intergovernmental Maritime Consultative Organization
Chancery House, Chancery Lane
London W.C. 2, England

This organization and its affiliate, the Internation Convention for the Prevention of Pollution of the Sea by Oil, will provide information on request.

Lake Carriers Association
305 Rockefeller Building
Cleveland, Ohio 44121
Tel: 216-621-1107

Provides brief information services on oil pollution of the Great Lakes. Also provides limited advisory services.

Louisiana Geological Survey
Box G, University Station
Baton Rouge, La. 70803
Tel: 504-389-5812

Concerned with ground water problems and protection of fresh-water sands against pollution by drilling and oil and gas wells. Provides information or suggests specialists for consultation.

National Marine Water Quality Laboratory
Federal Water Quality Administration
U. S. Department of the Interior
Liberty Lane at Fairgrounds Road
P. O. Box 277
West Kingston, R.I. 02892
Tel: 401-789-9738

Answers questions and provides reference and referral services to interested inquirers. Has done studies on pollution of marine waters by oil.

National Petroleum Refiners Association
1725 De Sales Street, N.W., Suite 802
Washington, D.C. 20036
Tel: 202-638-3722

Has prepared studies on petroleum refiners' part in the control of oil pollution. Conducts surveys on this problem. Publications include a newsletter, proceedings, and special manuals.

Oil Spill Information Center
Sciences-Engineering Library
University of California at Santa Barbara
Santa Barbara, Calif. 93106
Tel: 805-961-3948

Serves as clearinghouse for information on oil spills. Maintains a registry of experts. Supports legislation for the control of oil spills. Permits onsite use of the collection.

Public Information Office
U. S. Maritime Administration
441 G Street, N.W., Room 3037
Washington, D.C. 20235
Tel: 202-967-2746

Answers questions on pollution by oil of marine waters, as well as oil pollution control. Most of materials are free on request in single copies. Supplies photographs without charge for use in publications.

St. Lawrence Seaway Development Corporation
U. S. Department of Transportation
Seaway Circle
Massena, N.Y. 13662
Tel: 315-764-0271

Concerned with hydropower, water transportation, and the regulation of oil pollution on the Seaway. Provides information upon request.

Pesticides

Chemical Abstracts Service
American Chemical Society
2041 North College Road
Columbus, Ohio 43210
Tel: 614-293-5022

This service provides answers to technical questions and performs literature searches. Fees vary according to the nature and complexity of the request. It prepares *Chemical Abstracts,* biweekly, published and sold by the American Chemical Society, 1155 16th Street, N.W., Washington, D.C. 20006.

Director of Information
Tennessee Valley Authority
New Sparkle Building
Knoxville, Tenn. 37902
Tel: 615-522-7181

The office answers, free of charge, questions related to insects and insect control.

Information Unit
Division of Community Studies
Food and Drug Administration CP&EHS
U.S. Public Health Service
4770 Buford Highway

Chamblee, Ga. 30341
Tel: 404-633-3311, Ext. 5201

Assesses the total impact of pesticides upon human health. Collects and disseminates information on environmental health research. Publishes *Health Aspects of Pesticides Abstracts Bulletin* and its *Pesticides Monitoring Journal.*

Military Entomology Information Service
Armed Forces Pest Control Board
Forest Glen Section
Walter Reed Army Medical Center
Washington, D.C. 20012
Tel: 202-576-5365

Collects and disseminates information concerning the medical and engineering aspects of military entomology, to exclude agricultural entomology and forest coverage. Resource is limited to pesticides and venoms. Answers specific questions directly, or by means of bibliographic citations. Provides consulting services to other federal agencies and approved researchers.

National Agricultural Chemicals Association
1155 15th Street, N.W.
Washington, D.C. 20005
Tel: 202-296-1585

Conducts research to improve the quality of chemicals and to discover new chemicals for agricultural uses. Publishes *NAC News and Pesticide Review,* bimonthly, with an annual issue concerning U.S. FDA tolerances. Answers inquiries and provides consulting and advisory services.

National Agricultural Library
U.S. Department of Agriculture
Beltsville, Md. 20705
Tel: 202-345-6200, Ext. 263

Open to the public, the Library answers questions and provides references within its time available for free service. The Library lends monographs on an interlibrary loan basis and sells photoreproductions of its holdings. *Library Lists,* subject bibliographies prepared as an aid to Department programs, are available for free limited distribution. Publishes *Pesticide Documentation Bulletin,* a biweekly index.

Office of the Secretary
Association of American Pesticide Control Officials, Inc.
1615 South Harrison Road
East Lansing, Mich. 48823
Tel: 517-332-0885, Ext. 2605

Provides answers to technical questions or makes referrals to those who can. Primarily concerned with pesticide chemicals, their sale and distribution data, and the enforcement of related laws. Limited services available, due to small staff. Publishes *Pesticide Chemicals Official Compendium.*

Pesticides Analysis Research Center
Midwest Research Institute
425 Volker Boulevard
Kansas City, Mo. 64110
Tel: 816-561-0202

Primarily performing research on analytical methods for pesticides, in formulations and as residues in all types of samples, including foodstuffs, soils, air, water, vegetation, and tissues. Charges fees, except for simple questions.

Pesticides Regulation Division (ARS)
U.S. Department of Agriculture
Washington, D.C. 20250
Tel: 202-388-4267

Answers inquiries on registered pesticide chemicals. Reviews safety and efficacy data submitted by applicants for registration of pesticide chemicals. Answers letter inquiries from allied professionals concerning registered products.

Western Pesticides Research Laboratory
Food and Drug Administration
P. O. Box 73
Wenatchee, Wash. 98801
Tel: 509-663-8511, Ext. 331

Answers inquiries for information on pesticides and their effects on humans, protection from exposure to pesticides, air sampling, and analytical methods.

Population

Center for Migration Studies
209 Flagg Place
Staten Island, N.Y. 10304
Tel: 212-357-0232

Primarily concerned with the sociological, psychological, and historical problems of migration.

General Secretariat
International Union for the Scientific Study of Population
23 Avenue Franklin Roosevelt
Paris 8e, France

Sponsors scientific investigations of population problems and has sponsored the International Population Conference. Issues *Le Demographe,* periodically, and other related publications.

International Census Bureau Project
Department of Demography
University of California

Appendix C

Building T-8, Room 213
Berkeley, Calif.
Tel: 415-642-6412

Maintains a foreign populations census collection and provides information on the location of foreign population censuses for serious scholars.

Office of Population Research
Princeton University
5 Ivy Lane
Princeton, N.J. 08540
Tel: 609-452-4870

Engages in all aspects of demographic research, with emphasis on international studies of the interrelation of social, economic, and population change. Conducts research on problems of population in both qualitative and quantitative aspects. Assists in publication of *Population Index* with the Population Association of America on a quarterly basis. *Population Index* is an annotated bibliography of books and periodical literature on all phases of population problems. The office also maintains a library open to anyone. Reference service is available free, time permitting.

Population Association of America
P. O. Box 14182, Ben Franklin Station
Washington, D.C. 20044
Tel: 202-393-3253

Is interested in spatial distribution of population, trends in size, mortality, fertility, etc.; internal and international migration; demographic health and political factors; population control; methods and research analysis. Publishes *Demography,* an annual journal based largely on papers presented at the Associations's annual meeting, and *Population Index,* a detailed bibliography, in conjunction with the Office of Population Research.

Population Council
245 Park Avenue
New York, N.Y. 10017
Tel: 212-687-8330

Worldwide clearinghouse concerned with scientific information in the broad field of population. Helps support various research and pilot projects on population problems throughout the world. Consulting and documentary services are available primarily to U.S. and foreign government agencies, to private associations and academic institutions.

Population Crisis Committee
1730 K Street, N.W.
Washington, D.C. 20006
Tel: 202-659-1833

Provides information on the problems related to population, and publishes a newsletter and pamphlets which are available upon request.

Population Division
Bureau of the Census
Washington, D.C. 20233

Information on various aspects of population are provided by the following Sections:

Statistical Information Branch (Population & Housing)
Tel: 301-440-1202

Estimates and Projections
Tel: 301-440-7038

International Demographic Center
Tel: 301-440-7757

Foreign Demographic Analysis
Tel: 301-443-8675

Demographic Surveys (Scientific aspects of population and demography)
Tel: 301-440-1204

Population Reference Bureau, Inc.
1755 Massachusetts Avenue, N.W.
Washington, D.C. 20036
Tel: 202-232-2288

Gathers, interprets and distributes data on world and regional phenomena. Has information on population legislation and acts as a clearinghouse for population information. Prime concern is demographic forecasting, characterization of developing countries, etc.

Population Research Center
Bureau of Business Research
University of Texas
Business Economics Building
Austin, Tex. 78712
Tel: 512-471-1616

Although primarily concerned with business research and all aspects of the economy of the state of Texas, the center has published the *International Population Census Bibliography: Latin America and the Caribbean, 1965–*.

Scripps Foundation for Research in Population Problems
218 Harrison Hall
Miami University
Oxford, Ohio 45056
Tel: 513-523-2161, Ext. 671

Publishes numerous reports dealing with population problems, demography, etc., with special reference to fertility trends and differentials, migration and population growth in the U.S., immigration, human mortality, vital statistics, and human ecology.

Appendix C

Statistical Office
Department of Economic and Social Affairs
United Nations
New York, N.Y. 10017
Tel: 212-754-1234

Collects information on world population and publishes the *Demographic Yearbook*. Provides free reference and referral service and publications as priced. *Bibliography of Recent Official Demographic Statistics,* Statistical paper series M no.18, $80.00 (Part 1 and 2).

The following publication may provide additional information:

Selected References on Relocation, published by and available from the National Association of Housing and Redevelopment Officials, 2600 Virginia Avenue, N.W., Washington, D.C. 20037. $1.50 to non-members. (Latest edition: May, 1967)

Solid Wastes

Albany Metallurgy Research Center
U.S. Bureau of Mines
P.O. Box 70
West Queen Avenue
Albany, Oreg. 97321
Tel: 503-926-5811

Performs research on the production of metals. Has special projects on the recovery of metals from industrial wastes and scrap metal products. Provides information as time and regulations permit.

Aluminum Smelters Research Institute
20 North Wacker Drive
Chicago, Ill. 60606
Tel: 312-726-1475

Sponsors research and provides information on the recovery of aluminum from scrap. Services are primarily to sponsors, to others as time and regulations permit.

Bureau of Solid Waste Management
Environmental Health Service
U.S. Public Health Service
12720 Twinbrook Parkway
Rockville, Md. 20852
Tel: 301-443-3224

Sponsors research on solid waste disposal. Provides information and suggests cooperating scientists and facilities for consultation.

Bureau of Solid Waste Management
Environmental Health Service
U.S. Public Health Service
222 East Central Parkway
Cincinnati, Ohio 45402
Tel: 513-871-1820

Answers brief inquiries and provides consultation and advice to organizational members.

Department of Environmental Systems Engineering
Clemson University
Lowry Hall
Clemson, S.C. 29631
Tel: 803-654-2421, Ext. 272

Performs research on the disposal of waste, primarily of solid wastes. Provides information and consultation as time permits.

Disposal Group
Society of the Plastics Industry, Inc.
250 Park Avenue
New York, N.Y. 10017
Tel: 212-687-2675

Provides information and advice on the disposal of plastic materials. Suggests cooperating members for extensive consultation.

Division of Environmental Research and Development
U.S. Tennessee Valley Authority
11th and Market Streets (Edney Building)
Chattanooga, Tenn. 37401
Tel: 615-755-2002

Performs research on solid wastes disposal, dust, flyash, etc. Provides information and consultation on request.

Energy Research Center
U.S. Bureau of Mines
4800 Forbes Avenue
Pittsburgh, Pa. 15213
Tel: 412-892-2400

Performs research on the conversion of municipal and industrial refuse into useful materials by pyrolysis. Provides information and document services on request.

Environmental Pollution Center
Midwest Research Institute
425 Volker Boulevard
Kansas City, Mo. 64110
Tel: 816-561-0202

Performs research on a contract basis. Consultation and extensive reference services are provided for a fee.

Incinerator Committee
Process Industries Division
American Society of Mechanical Engineers
345 East 42nd Street
New York, N.Y. 10017
Tel: 212-752-6800

Sponsors conferences on the disposal of solid wastes. Provides information or directs inquirers to cooperating members and facilities.

Incinerator Institute of America
60 E. 42nd Street
New York, N.Y. 10017
Tel: 212-687-0994

Provides information and consultation on incinerators and solid waste disposal. Literature references and publications are sold for a fee.

Institute of Solid Wastes
American Public Works Association
1313 East 60th Street
Chicago, Ill. 60637
Tel: 312-324-3400

Provides document and consulting services to its members. Publishes and sells reports, standards, conference proceedings, and other materials.

Keep America Beautiful, Inc.
99 Park Avenue
New York, N.Y. 10016
Tel: 212-682-4546

Acts as clearinghouse for litter prevention techniques, methods, and materials information.

National Association of Secondary Material Industries
330 Madison Avenue
New York, N.Y. 10017
Tel: 212-867-7330

Sponsors research and provides information and consultation on the re-use of solid waste materials. Suggests cooperating members for consultation on questions which cannot be answered by the Association.

National Environmental Health Association
1550 Lincoln Street
Denver, Colo. 80203
Tel: 303-222-4456

Provides information and consultation. Publishes the *Journal of Environmental*

Health. Conducts annual education conferences and provides employment and placement services for its members.

Rubber Reclaimers Association
101 West 31st Street
New York, N.Y. 10001
Tel: 212-736-6872

Provides information or refers inquiries to special committees or cooperating members.

Salt Lake City Metallurgy Research Center
U.S. Bureau of Mines
1600 East 1st South Street
Salt Lake City, Utah 84112
Tel: 801-524-5350

Performs research on special metals. Maintains a research program on the recovery of useful products from solid industrial wastes and scrap automobiles. Provides information as time permits.

Scrap Rubber and Plastics Institute
National Association of Secondary Materials Industries
330 Madison Avenue
New York, N.Y. 10017
Tel: 212-867-7330

Provides services primarily to members, to others as time permits.

Technical Association of the Pulp and Paper Industry
360 Lexington Avenue
New York, N.Y. 10017
Tel: 212-682-8313

Answers technical questions or refers inquiries to qualified members. Publishes *TAPPI,* monthly, and the annual *Bibliography of Papermaking in the US.*
Has special committees on the deinking of paper and the re-use and disposal of waste paper.

Thermal Pollution

Bureau of Sanitary Engineering
Pennsylvania State Department of Health
P.O. Box 90
Harrisburg, Pa. 17120
Tel: 717-787-4660

Has studied the problem of thermal pollution in Pennsylvania rivers and can provide information and documents.

Appendix C

Department of Civil Engineering
University of Pittsburgh
325 Engineering Hall
Pittsburgh, Pa. 15213
Tel: 412-621-3500

Performs research on water problems including thermal contamination. Maintains a reference library for its use and interlibrary loan services. Its research facilities include computer centers.

IDRES Information Center
Franklin Institute Research Laboratories
Benjamin Franklin Parkway at 20th Street
Philadelphia, Pa. 19103
Tel: 215-448-1485

The Center is connected with the Institute for the Development of Riverine and Estuarine Systems (IDRES) and provides information and document services in accordance with regulations.

Illinois State Water Survey
P.O. Box 232
Urbana, Ill. 61802
Tel: 217-333-2210

Concerned with groundwater and surfacewater hydrology; pollution, including thermal contamination; biological environments; etc. It answers technical questions and makes referrals to cooperating specialists. Its extensive library is open for onsite reference.

Institute of Paper Chemistry
P.O. Box 1048
Appleton, Wis. 54911
Tel: 414-734-9251

The Institute is concerned with industry related problems of waste and its treatment, thermal pollution, treatment of industrial water supply, etc. Its library is open to the public. Services are generally free of charge or provided at cost.

Institute of Water Resources
University of Connecticut
Storrs, Conn. 06268
Tel: 203-429-9321, Ext. 474

Performs research on all aspects of the hydrologic cycle, including pollution and the reduction of river heat pollution. Staff members provide information or make referrals.

Maryland Geological Survey
214 Latrobe Hall
The Johns Hopkins University
Baltimore, Md. 21218
Tel: 301-235-0771

Fields of interest include groundwater and surfacewater hydrology, run-off, sedimentation, geological environment of lakes, thermal contamination, etc. The Survey maintains open-file information for public use and provides information on request.

National Coal Policy Conference, Inc.
1000 16th Street, N.W.
Washington, D.C. 20036
Tel: 212-783-4751

Has sponsored research on aquatic thermal pollution and its implications (by the Travelers Research Corporation, 250 Constitution Plaza, Hartford, Conn. 06103) and has published the results. Copies of the reports are available from the Conference.

Pacific Northwest Water Laboratory
U.S. Federal Water Quality Administration
501 Pittock Block
Portland, Oreg. 97205
Tel: 503-752-4281

Has performed research and published an *Industrial Waste Guide on Thermal Pollution* (1968). Provides information and consultation as time permits.

Subcommittee on Air and Water Pollution
Senate Committee on Public Works
U.S. Congress
Washington, D.C. 20510
Tel: 202-225-6176

Has held hearings on thermal pollution and can provide pertinent documents.

Water Resources Research Center
University of Maryland
Shriver Laboratory
College Park, Md. 20740
Tel: 301-454-3901

Performs research including computer simulation of water resources regimes, effects of thermal pollution on estuarine waters, etc. Provides information as time and regulations permit.

Water Resources Research Institute
Oregon State University
114 Covell Hall
Oregon State University
Corvallis, Oreg. 97331
Tel: 503-754-1023

The Institute performs research on all aspects of water, including pollution, thermal, pesticide, and radioactive. Staff members provide information or suggest other specialists for consultation.

Appendix C

Urban Affairs

Housing

International Federation for Housing and Planning
43 Wassenaarseweg
The Hague, The Netherlands

Maintains information, documentation, and library services which are available to public authorities, professional organizations, and individual specialists concerning housing and town planning.

National Association of Housing and Redevelopment Officials
2600 Virginia Avenue, N.W.
Washington, D.C. 20037
Tel: 202-333-2020

Provides information on housing and urban renewal and development. Publishes the *Journal of Housing,* monthly, and the *Housing and Urban Renewal Directory,* every two to three years. Brief questions answered free, more extensive consultation for members only.

Small Home Council—Building Research Council
University of Illinois
One East St. Mary's Road
Champaign, Ill. 61820
Tel: 217-333-1801, Ext. 457

Collects information on construction methods and materials, design and space utilization for single family housing. Answers questions and gives information concerning current research and development projects. Advisory and consulting services are provided for a fee.

Library, U.S. Department of Housing and Urban Development
451 7th Street, S.W., Room 8140
Washington, D.C. 20410
Tel: 202-755-6370

Has consolidated with the Federal Housing Administration Library and the Housing Assistance Administration Library to form a single HUD Library. Permits onsite reference and makes interlibrary loans. Answers brief inquiries and provides literature searches for a fee. Publishes *Housing and Planning References,* a monthly index to urban literature which is available by subscription from the Superintendent of Documents, Government Printing Office, Washington, D.C. 20402.

Urban Affairs

Information Center
U.S. Department of Housing and Urban Development
451 7th Street, S.W., Room 1202

108

Washington, D.C. 20410
Tel: 202-755-6420

Answers questions and refers requests to the appropriate offices with the Department of Housing and Urban Development. Answers questions on on-going projects administered by the Department.

National League of Cities
1612 K Street, N.W.
Washington, D.C. 20006
Tel: 202-293-7300

Answers inquiries, provides advisory and consulting services, and permits onsite use of its collections on materials on public administration and urban government. Publishes *Nation's Cities,* monthly.

National Urban League
55 East 52nd Street
New York, N.Y. 10022
Tel: 212-751-0300

Answers inquiries and provides reference and literature searching services on those subjects clearly related to the urban areas. Sells bibliographies on urban problems, housing, etc.

Urban Development and Urban Renewal

The Urban Land Institute
1200 18th Street, N.W.
Washington, D.C. 20036
Tel: 202-338-6800

Provides answers to technical inquiries, furnishes advisory and consulting services, and refers inquirers to other organizations or specialists. Publishes *Urban Land,* monthly; *Land Use News Letter;* and numerous others. Also prepares short lists of literature citations.

Urban Studies Library
Kent State University
Room 252, Lowry Hall
Kent, Ohio 44240
Tel: 216-672-2002

Answers inquiries and provides abstracting and indexing services. Maintains an automatic urban and regional bibliographical information system (URBIS) which now contains approximately 13,000 abstracts. URBIS services are for a fee to customers.

Urban Planning

American Institute of Planners
917 15th Street, N.W., Room 800

Washington, D.C. 20005
Tel: 202-783-0666

Provides information and reference services on a limited scale primarily to members, but to others when time and staff permits. Refers inquiries to other specialists or organizations. Publishes *AIP Journal,* bimonthly.

American Society of Planning Officials
1313 East 60th Street
Chicago, Ill. 60637
Tel: 312-324-3400

Answers inquiries and provides research information and advice on planning, zoning, land use, and allied subjects. Provides consulting services on a contract basis. Publishes *Planning Advisory Service Reports,* monthly, and *Zoning Digest,* monthly. Extended services available to subscribers only.

Downtown Ideas Exchange
125 East 23rd Street
New York, N.Y. 10010
Tel: 212-473-7003

Provides consulting services for a fee and publications by subscription. Publishes *Downtown Ideas Exchange,* semi-monthly, and other periodicals and miscellaneous materials in this subject area. Consulting services are provided under the firm name of Alexander and Moskowitz, Inc.

International City Managers Association
1140 Connecticut Avenue, N.W.
Washington, D.C. 20036
Tel: 202-293-2200

Provides advisory and consulting services free of charge. Provides reference services in all aspects of urban planning, development, and other subjects related to urban affairs and public administration. Publishes *Urban Data Service,* annually.

Water Pollution Control

Government Resources

Association of State and Interstate Water Pollution Control Administrators
P.O. Box 11143
Richmond, Va. 23230
Tel: 703-770-2241

Provides information on state and interstate activities in water pollution control. Provides referral services to various state officials.

Bureau of Water Hygiene
National Center for Urban & Industrial Health
U.S. Environmental Control Administration

222 East Central Parkway
Cincinnati, Ohio 45202
Tel: 513-684-3571

Answers inquiries on protection of waters polluted by various means. Concerned with health aspects of water pollution control. Provides references and makes referrals.

Committee on Merchant Marine and Fisheries
U.S. Congress. House of Representatives
Room 1334, Longworth House Office Building
Washington, D.C. 20515
Tel: 202-225-4047

Answers questions and provides services in the form of Committee prints and various publications on water pollution control, including legislation. Covers water pollution and its effects on marine life.

Committee on Public Works
U.S. Congress. House of Representatives
Room 2165, Rayburn House Office Building
Washington, D.C. 20515
Tel: 202-225-4472

Answers questions and provides services in the form of Committee prints and various publications on water pollution control, including legislation.

Committee on Public Works
U.S. Congress. Senate
Room 4204, New Senate Office Building
Washington, D.C. 20510
Tel: 202-225-6176

Answers questions and provides services in the form of Committee prints and various publications on water pollution. Has also available a film for loan or sale entitled *Troubled Waters.*

Environmental Hygiene Agency
Office of the Surgeon General
U.S. Department of the Army
Edgewood Arsenal, Md. 21010
Tel: 301-671-4236

Answers questions and provides other services to military and government agency personnel on environmental health and hygiene. Provides data on water pollution control measures for health.

New England Interstate Water Pollution Control Commission
73 Tremont Street, Room 950
Boston, Mass. 02108
Tel: 617-742-0281

Answers questions and provides referral services concerning water pollution control activities in the six New England states region. Publishes an annual report and a newsletter. Has maps, charts, and photographs available for onsite use.

Office of Public Information
U.S. Federal Water Quality Administration
Washington, D.C. 20242
Tel: 703-557-7373

Answers inquiries, provides consulting and limited reference services, provides bibliographic citations and abstracts, and makes referrals. Makes available in many forms all IWGA research and development efforts.

Technical Library
U.S. Tennessee Valley Authority
500 Union Avenue, S.W.
Knoxville, Tenn. 37902
Tel: 615-522-7181

Answers inquiries, provides materials for interlibrary loan on the TVA's efforts in the field of water pollution control. Publishes three annual bibliographies on its activities.

Water Resources Division
Geological Survey
U.S. Department of the Interior
18th and F Streets, N.W.
Washington, D.C. 20242
Tel: 202-343-3595

Answers inquiries on water quality, including water pollution and pollution control. Makes references to Geological Survey publications.

Water Resources and Engineering Services Division
Bureau of Domestic Commerce
U.S. Department of Commerce
14th Street and Constitution Avenue, N.W.
Washington, D.C. 20230
Tel: 202-967-4347

Provides assistance to industries and individuals concerning various programs in water pollution control, but especially to engineers.

Private Organizations

American Public Health Association
1740 Broadway
New York, N.Y. 10019
Tel: 212-245-8000

Publishes *Standard Methods for the Examination of Water and Waste Water* (12th ed., 1965).

American Society of Sanitary Engineering
228 Standard Building
Cleveland, Ohio 44113
Tel: 216-621-8520

Answers questions and provides reference and referral services on control of water pollution for sanitary conditions. Provides services especially to sanitary engineers.

American Water Resources Association
P.O. Box 434
Urbana, Ill. 61801
Tel: 217-367-9695

Publishes and sells *Water Resources Abstracts,* monthly; *Hydata,* annually. Provides a *Hydata Reader Service* which furnishes papers or abstracts indexed in *Hydata.*

American Water Works Association
2 Park Avenue
New York, N.Y. 10016
Tel: 212-686-2040

Collects and disseminates information on water, water technology, water treatment, and related fields. Publishes its *Journal* monthly.

Committee D-19 on Water
American Society for Testing and Materials
1916 Race Street
Philadelphia, Pa. 19103
Tel: 215-569-4200

Develops test methods; provides information through its publications.

IDRES Information Center
(Institute for the Development of Riverine and Estuarine Systems)
Science Information Services
Franklin Institute Research Laboratories
Benjamin Franklin Parkway at 20th Street
Philadelphia, Pa. 19103
Tel: 215-448-1485

Provides information services for a fee depending on time and staff involved. Distributes publications on water pollution control activities in river and estuary systems.

National Council of the Paper Industry for Air and Stream Improvement
103 Park Avenue
New York, N.Y. 10017
Tel: 212-889-5416

Answers questions and provides services in the form of its publications including *Monthly Bulletin, Regulatory Review,* and other varied reports.

Appendix C

National Water Institute
744 Broad Street, Room 3405
Newark, N.J. 07102
Tel: 201-623-1727

Serves as the public relations arm of the Water and Wastewater Equipment Manufacturers Association. Answers questions and provides pamphlets and booklets on water pollution control.

U.S. National Committee
International Association on Water Pollution Research
3900 Wisconsin Avenue, N.W.
Washington, D.C. 20016
Tel: 202-362-4100, Ext. 3741

Answers inquiries on U.S. Committee's activities in relations to the International community on water pollution control progress and projects.

Water Conditioning Research Council
325 West Wesley Street
P.O. Box 651
Wheaton, Ill. 60187
Tel: 312-668-8892

Cosponsored by the Water Conditioning Association International and the Association of Water Conditioning Equipment Manufacturers. Answers questions and provides referral services in the field of water pollution control.

Water Information Center, Inc.
Water Research Building, Manorhaven
Port Washington, N.Y. 11050
Tel: 516-883-6780

Answers questions and provides consulting services for a fee. Publishes *Water Newsletter,* semimonthly; *Research and Development News,* monthly; *Water Atlas of the United States;* and *Water Encyclopedia.* All publications are for sale by the Center.

Water Pollution Control Federation
3900 Wisconsin Avenue, N.W.
Washington, D.C. 20016
Tel: 202-362-4100

Answers questions free of charge and provides reference, referral, advisory, and consulting services. Publishes *Journal: Water Pollution Control Federation,* monthly. Permits onsite use of collection by appointment.

Appendix
D

Organizations Concerned About Environmental Problems

American Association for the Advancement of Science
1515 Massachusetts Avenue, N.W.
Washington, D.C. 20005

American Association of Botanical Gardens and Aboretums
c/o Francis DeVos
Chicago Botanical Garden
116 South Michigan Avenue
Chicago, Ill. 60603

American Association of Zoological Parks and Aquariums
Oglebay Park
Wheeling, W.Va. 26003

American Forestry Association
919 17th Street, N.W.
Washington, D.C. 20006

American Institute of Architects
1735 New York Avenue, N.W.
Washington, D.C. 20006

American Institute of Biological Sciences
3900 Wisconsin Avenue, N.W.
Washington, D.C. 20016

American Institute of Planners
917 15th Street, N.W.
Washington, D.C. 20005

Appendix D

American Littoral Society
Sandy Hook
Highlands, N.J. 07732

American Museum Association
Smithsonian Institution
Washington, D.C. 20020

American Nature Study Society
c/o William Stapp
1501 Granada
Ann Arbor, Mich. 48103

American Planning and Civic Association
901 Union Trust Building
Washington, D.C. 20005

American Society for Range Management
2120 South Birch Street
Denver, Colo. 80222

American Society of Agronomy
677 Segoe Road
Madison, Wis. 537111

American Society of Ichthyologists and Herpetologists
c/o Charles Walker
Museum of Zoology
University of Michigan
Ann Arbor, Mich. 48104

American Society of Landscape Architects
2013 Eye Street, N.W.
Washington, D.C. 20006

American Society of Limnology and Oceanography
c/o F. Ronald Hayes
Fisheries Research Board of Canada
Ottawa, Ontario, Canada

American Society of Mammalogists
c/o Richard Van Gelder
American Museum of Natural History
Central Park W. at 79th Street
New York, N.Y. 10024

American Society of Planning Officials
1313 E. 60th Street
Chicago, Ill. 60637

Appalachian Trail Conference
1718 N Street, N.W.
Washington, D.C. 20006

Association of American Geographers
1146 16th Street, N.W.
Washington, D.C. 20036

Association of Conservation Engineers
c/o Don Hays
Department of Fish and Wildlife Resources
State Office Building Annex
Frankfort, Ky. 40601

Association of Consulting Foresters
Box 6
Wake, Va. 23176

California Roadside Council
2626 Ocean Avenue
San Francisco, Calif. 94132

California Tomorrow
Monadnock Building
681 Market Street
San Francisco, Calif. 94105

Citizens for Clean Air
40 W. 57th Street
New York, N.Y. 10019

Citizens League against the Sonic Boom
19 Appleton Street
Cambridge, Mass. 02138

Colorado Open Space Council
5850 E. Jewell Avenue
Denver, Colo. 80222

Conservation Education Association
1250 Connecticut Avenue, N.W.
Washington, D.C. 20036

Conservation Foundation
1250 Connecticut Avenue, N.W.
Washington, D.C. 20036

Conservation Law Society of America
Mills Tower
220 Bush Street
San Francisco, Calif. 94104

Defenders of Wildlife
1346 Connecticut Avenue, N.W.
Washington, D.C. 20036

Desert Protective Council
P.O. Box 33
Banning, Calif. 92220

Ducks, Unlimited
P.O. Box 66300
Chicago, Ill. 60666

Ecological Society of America
c/o John Cantlon
Department of Botany
Michigan State University
East Lansing, Mich. 48823

Federation of Western Outdoor Clubs
c/o Betty Hughes
Route 3
Box 172
Carmel, Calif. 93921

Friends of the Earth
451 Pacific Avenue
San Francisco, Calif. 94133

Garden Clubs of America
598 Madison Avenue
New York, N.Y. 10022

International Shade Tree Conference
1827 Neil Avenue
Columbus, Ohio 43210

Massachusetts Audubon Society
South Great Road
Lincoln, Mass. 01776

National Academy of Sciences
2101 Constitution Avenue, N.W.
Washington, D.C.

National Association of Soil and Water Conservation Districts
1025 Vermont Avenue, N.W.
Washington, D.C. 20005

National Audubon Society
1130 Fifth Avenue
New York, N.Y. 10038

National Council of State Garden Clubs
4401 Magnolia Avenue
St. Louis, Mo. 63110

National Parks Association
1701 18th Street, N.W.
Washington, D.C. 20009

National Recreation and Park Association
1700 Pennsylvania Avenue, N.W.
Washington, D.C. 20006

National Science for Youth Foundation
114 East 30th Street
New York, N.Y. 10016

National Speleological Society
203 Virginia Hills Avenue
Alexandria, Va.

National Trust for Historic Preservation
Decatur House
748 Jackson Place, N.W.
Washington, D.C. 20006

National Wildlife Federation
1412 16th Street, N.W.
Washington, D.C.

The Nature Conservancy
1522 K Street, N.W.
Washington, D.C.

Open Lands Project
123 W. Madison Street
Chicago, Ill. 60602

Open Space Institute
145 East 52nd Street
New York, N.Y. 10022

Outdoor Writers' Association of America
Outdoors Building
Columbia, Mo. 65201

Planned Parenthood
515 Madison Avenue
New York, N.Y. 10022

Regional Plan Association
230 W. 41st Street
New York, N.Y. 10036

Resources for the Future
1145 19th Street, N.W.
Washington, D.C. 20006

Save-the-Redwoods League
114 Sansome Street
San Francisco, Calif. 94104

Scientists' Institute for Public Information
30 East 68th Street
New York, N.Y. 10021

Society of American Foresters
1010 16th Street, N.W.
Washington, D.C.

Soil Conservation Society of America
835 5th
Des Moines, Iowa 50309

Sport Fishing Institute
719 13th Street, N.W.
Washington, D.C. 20005

Trout Unlimited
2526 State Street
P.O. Box 1807
Saginaw, Mich. 48605

Urban America
1717 Massachusetts Avenue, N.W.
Washington, D.C. 20036

Western Pennsylvania Conservancy
204 Fifth Avenue
Pittsburgh, Pa. 15222

The Wilderness Society
729 15th Street, N.W.
Washington, D.C. 20005

The Wildlife Society
3900 Wisconsin Avenue, N.W.
Washington, D.C. 20016

Appendix
E

National Ecology Centers

Pratt Remmel
Arkansas Ecology Center
316 Chester St.
Little Rock, Ark. 72201
501-374-6271

Pat Shaylor
Ecology Center
2179 Alliston Way
Berkeley, Calif. 94074

Dave Richardson
South County Ecology Center
3667 Castro Valley Blvd.
Castro Valley, Calif. 94578
415-582-4776

Eve Rooser
Valley Ecology Center
Suite 223
119 South Livermore Ave.
Livermore, Calif. 94550
415-443-5483

Dick Whitehead
National Ecology Foundation
335 N. San Antonio Rd.
Los Altos, Calif. 94022
415-941-3406

Marcia Fowler
Peninsula Conservation Center
Box 548
Menlo Park, Calif.
415-322-6671

Cliff Humphrey
Ecology Action Educational Institute
Box 3895
Modesto, Calif. 95352
209-529-3784

Kurt Meckenson
Ecology Information Center
4641 Marceni Ave.
Sacramento, Calif. 95821
916-482-6664

Pat Heffernan
Marin Ecology Center
Box 725
San Anselmo, Calif. 94960

Gil Baile
San Francisco Ecology Center
Sunflower Bookstore
711 Montgomery St.
San Francisco, Calif. 94111
415-391-7664

Ray Balter
Ecology Center Press
10th and Howard
San Francisco, Calif.

Paul Relis
Community Ecology Center
15 West Anapamu St.
Santa Barbara, Calif. 93104
805-962-2210

Chuck Hinkle
The Environmental Center
211 Santa Rosa Ave.
Santa Rosa, Calif.
707-545-2196

George Coling
Environmental Resources
2000 P St., N.W.
Washington, D.C. 20036
202-293-6960

Bill Painter, Terry Sepher
Washington Ecology Center
3256 Prospect St., N.W.
Washington, D.C. 20007
202-338-5010

Ross Vincent, Wendell Dyer
Ecology Center of Louisiana
Box 15149
New Orleans, La. 70115
504-949-7612

Susan "Rabbit" Goody
Boston Area Ecology Action Center
925 Massachusetts Ave.
Cambridge, Mass. 02139
617-876-7085

Bill Kepper, George Coling
ENACT Ecology Center
417 Detroit St.
Ann Arbor, Mich. 48104
313-761-3186

Bob Nelson
Midwest Environmental Education
   and Research Association
   (MEERA)
1051 McKnight Rd.
St. Paul, Minn. 55119
612-735-4080

Stuart Leiderman
Environmental Response
Box 1124
Washington University
St. Louis, Mo. 63105
314-863-0100, Ext. 4070

Arnie Youngerman
Environment!
150 Fifth Ave.
New York, N.Y. 10011
212-673-8740

Dale Miller
40th St. Environmental Works
1401 NE 40th St.
Seattle, Wash. 98105
206-543-8700

Appendix
F

Environmental Protection Agency Regional Offices

Region I — Connecticut, Maine, Massachusetts, New Hampshire, Rhode Island, Vermont — Lester Klashman / Rm. 2303 / J.F. Kennedy Fed. Bldg. / Boston, Mass. 02203

Region II — New Jersey, New York, Puerto Rico, The Virgin Islands — Gerald M. Hansler / Rm. 847 / 26 Federal Plaza / New York, N.Y. 10007

Region III — Delaware, Maryland, Pennsylvania, Virginia, West Virginia, District of Columbia — Lloyd Gebhard / P.O. Box 12900 / Philadelphia, Pa. 19108

Region IV — Alabama, Florida, Georgia, Kentucky, Mississippi, North Carolina, South Carolina, Tennessee — John R. Thoman / Suite 300 / 1421 Peachtree St. NE / Atlanta, Ga. 30309

Region V — Illinois, Indiana, Michigan, Minnesota, Ohio, Wisconsin — Francis T. Mayo / 33 E. Congress Pkwy. / Chicago, Ill. 60605

Region VI — Arkansas, Louisiana, New Mexico, Texas, Oklahoma — Bill V. McFarland / 1114 Commerce St. / Dallas, Tex. 75202

Region VII	Iowa, Kansas, Missouri, Nebraska	John M. Rademacher Rm. 702 911 Walnut Street Kansas City, Mo. 64106
Region VIII	Colorado, Montana, North Dakota, South Dakota, Utah, Wyoming	Donald P. Dubois Rm. 9041 Federal Office Bldg. 19th and Stout St. Denver, Colo. 80202
Region IX	Arizona, California, Hawaii, Nevada, American Samoa, Guam, Trust Territories of Pacific Islands, Wake	Paul DeFalco, Jr. 760 Market St. San Francisco, Calif. 94102
Region X	Alaska, Idaho, Oregon, Washington	James L. Agee Rm. 501 Pittock Blk. 921 SW Washington St. Portland, Oreg. 97205